M000087228

THE
FIGHTING SHIP

Bernard Brett

Illustrated by John Batchelor and Ivan Lapper

Oxford University Press   1985

Oxford University Press, Walton Street, Oxford OX2 6DP

Oxford New York Toronto
Kuala Lumpur Singapore Hong Kong Tokyo
Delhi Bombay Calcutta Madras Karachi
Nairobi Dar es Salaam Cape Town
Melbourne Auckland

and associated companies in
Beirut Berlin Ibadan Mexico City Nicosia

Oxford is a trade mark of Oxford University Press
© Bernard Brett 1985

Brett, Bernard
 The Fighting Ship.
 1. Naval art and science – History
 I. Title
 359'.009   V27

 ISBN 0-19-273155-6

Phototypeset by Tradespools Ltd., Frome, Somerset
Printed in Hong Kong

Acknowledgements

The publishers would like to thank the following for permission to reproduce photographs:

Aldus Archive pp.36 (bottom right), 37 (top and bottom), 55 (centre), 65 (left); Blandford Press p.94–95 (left); British Library p.28 (left); Central Office of Information p.92 (below); Peter Connolly p.7; John Hamilton/Imperial War Museum pp.46–47, 68–69; Imperial War Museum pp.48, 76 (bottom); Marconi International Marine Co. Ltd. p.29 (centre); Marshall Cavendish Ltd., illustration: Sarson and Bryan p.71; Mary Evans Picture Library p.10; National Maritime Museum pp.11 (top and bottom), 15, 16–17, 24, 28 (right), 29 (three top right and bottom right), 45 (bottom); Royal Naval Museum, Portsmouth pp.23 (bottom), 39 (top right and bottom), 41, 42; Short Brothers Ltd. p.93 (bottom right); Siebe Gorman and Co. Ltd. p.77; United States, Department of the Navy p.64 (top); University of Oxford, Museum of the History of Science p.29 (top left); Vickers Shipbuilding and Engineering Ltd. p.88; Wayland Publishers Ltd. p.19.

Front Cover illustration is by Ivan Lapper
Back Cover illustrations are by John Batchelor
Maps drawn by Jeremy Cave

Contents

Armeinias of Pallene, Trierarch at Salamis, 480 BC   4

Romans to the fifteenth century   10

John Kidde, Gunner on *Revenge*, 1588   12

Midshipman Roberts aboard *Victory*
at Trafalgar, 1805   20

Navigation   28

Acting Assistant Paymaster, William Keeler,
aboard USS *Monitor*, 1862   30

The Battleship   36

'Lofty' Williams, Stoker First Class, aboard
HMS *Glasgow*, 1914   38

Herbert Hermann, Mechanikersobergefreiter, *U47*;
'Taffy' Davies, Corporal Marine,
HMS *Royal Oak*, 1939   44

Evolution of the Submarine   53

Sub-Lieutenant Wilson, Fleet Air Arm at
Matapan, 1941   56

Aircraft at Sea   64

Rheinübung: Exercise Rhine   66

Lieutenant-Captain Luigi de la Penne,
Alexandria, 1941   76

Commander Paul Bootherstone, HMS *Arrow*, 1982   84

Rank Insignia   94

International Code of Signals   95

Index   96

Armeinias of Pallene, Trierarch at Salamis, 480 BC

ARMEINIAS of Pallene, trierarch (Commander) of an Athenian trireme, huddled over the camp fire honing the edge of his cutting sword. It was long past midnight, but it was excitement rather than fear that had kept him awake that late September night in 480 BC. An hour ago he had left the Athenian Admiral's fireside, where Themistokles had revealed his daring plan to the assembled captains. According to Themistokles, the previous night his most trusted slave, Sikinnos, had been smuggled by boat across the straits from Salamis to Phalerum. There he was to tell the Persian king that the Greek fleet intended escaping under the cover of darkness the following night. Furthermore, if the Persian fleet were to enter the straits and boldly attack the Greeks, he, Themistokles, would desert to the Persians, taking with him his 200 Athenian ships. It remained to be seen if King Xerxes would be taken in.

The answer had come earlier in the evening, Areistides the Just, from Aegina, had arrived with the news that the Persian fleet was on the move. This had later been confirmed by Panaitios of Tenos, a trierarch, who, together with his crew had changed sides at the eleventh hour. The Persian fleet, over 1,000 galleys, was drawn up in three lines across the entrance to the straits; the Phoenician squadron on the right wing, the Ionians and other East Greeks on the left. Between them lay the island of Psyttaleia (Lipsokoutali). A commando of 400 nobles and picked troops had been landed to rescue any shipwrecked Persians and slaughter any Greeks who might be cast ashore during the battle. A powerful Egyptian squadron was racing up the west coast of Salamis to cut off the Greeks escaping to the north at Megara.

After a heated argument, the Athenians had been persuaded by the Congress of Greek States to abandon their city in favour of making a stand at the narrows of the Isthmus. This would be fortified and become the army's next line of defence against the Persian invaders. An oracle, forecast by Pythia, the priestess-announcer of the will of the god Apollo, at Delphi, had tipped the scales.

'Safe shall the wooden wall continue for thee and thy children.
Wait not the tramp of the horse, nor the footmen mightily moving
Over the land, but turn your back to the foe and retire ye.
Yet shall a day arrive when ye shall meet him in battle.
Holy Salamis, thou shall destroy the offspring of women,
When men scatter the seed, or when they gather the harvest.'

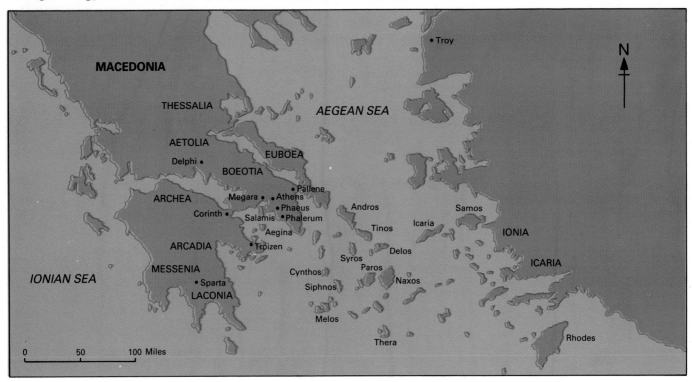

As no one knows for sure how the banks of oars were arranged on a trireme, over the centuries it has become a point of controversy among authorities. This has resulted in a number of conflicting systems being put forward: **A** Graser (1864) **B** Lemaitre (1883) **C** Busley (1919)

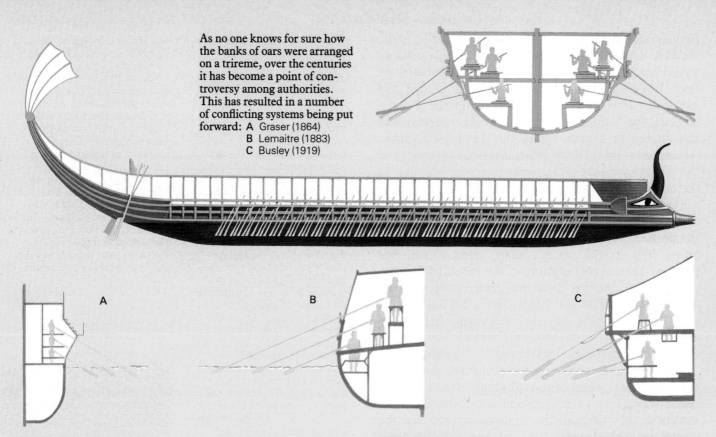

These two diagrams, showing the cross-section of a trireme, are constructed from the Athenian sculptured Lenormant relief of the period **D**, and the Talos vase drawing **E** – they appear to be identical.

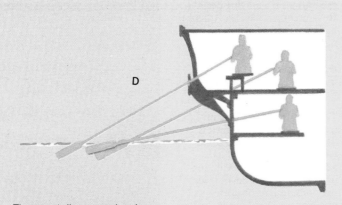

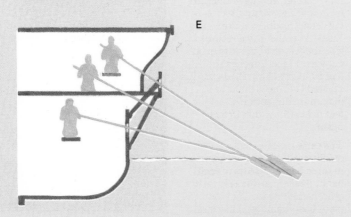

Warships of the Ancient World

The warship of the Eastern Mediterranean, built for speed, was a long, narrow, elegant galley with an upswept stern and a sharp ram at the bow. Although it carried a square sail, slung horizontally, this was only used when the wind was in the right direction – it was unshipped and stowed when the ship went into battle. The main propulsion source was oar-power. The ship usually beached at night, being dragged stern first up the shingle to ensure a swift launch and get-away in case of emergency.

Although Homer refers to black ships, the ships were often painted various colours above the waterline; below they were probably waterproofed with black pitch or tar. There is reference to an artist, Mimnes, painting a snake along the bulwark of a ship, in such a way that it appeared about to bite the helmsman. The ships that carried the Greeks to the Siege of Troy were most likely triakonters (30 oars, 15 each side) and pentekonters (50 oars, 25 each side), the oars set in a single bank. Made from pine wood they were propelled with oars of polished fir.

When more power was demanded from these narrow ships, the danger of 'hogging' (strain arching the keel of a vessel) and 'sagging' (a downward curving of the keel) made it impossible to lengthen the keel to increase the number of oars in a single bank. This led to the introduction of the bireme with its double bank of oars. Most probably introduced by the Phoenicians, it was about 80 feet long, with a 10 feet beam and a narrow fighting platform or deck running the whole length of the ship.

Each ship carried 10 marines, 4 archers, 15 deck hands and a flautist to pipe the beat for the oarsmen. They could probably reach speeds of 9 knots, covering long distances at an average speed of 4.5 knots.

Themistokles, son of Neokles, at the time of Salamis the most powerful man in Athens, had already turned the state into the strongest sea-power in Greece. As far back as 493 BC, when archon (the archon, or regent, was appointed to lead Athens for 1 year – by popular vote), he had persuaded the Assembly to fortify the peninsula of Piraeus and use its natural harbours as the Athenian naval base. Before they had hauled their ships on to the open beaches of Phalerum, where they were vulnerable to surprise attack by the Persian fleet.

5

Armeinias, like all other Greeks, firmly believed in the Delphic Oracle, the outcome of tomorrow's battle would surely prove him right – but 380 galleys against over 1,000? A small garrison, left to defend the Acropolis above the city, had held up the Persian advance for a fortnight, finally being overrun and slaughtered to a man. From the shores of Salamis, Armeinias and his fellow Athenians had sadly watched the pillars of smoke rising from their beloved city, as the enemy set it ablaze and desecrated the temples.

He looked down the length of the beach; from the town of Salamis northwards, Greek camp fires marked the position of each beached ship. His own stretched below him to the water's edge, stern awash, her polished bronze ram glinting in the moonlight, a few yards beyond the fire. Sleek and graceful, she was 110 feet long with an 18 feet beam. He lay his head on his shield and wrapping himself in his cloak, drifted into an uneasy sleep. About him were sprawled his crew of 200: rowers, marines, archers and deckhands.

He was shaken awake by the helmsman, it was still dark, but the sky had begun to lighten in the east. The beach was a hive of activity and noise; the shouts of rowers as they dragged the triremes into the sea, the crunch of keels through the sand, the plaintive notes of flutes, eerie in the pre-dawn darkness. Whilst the rowers got the galleys afloat, shipped the oars and gently paddled to keep the triremes steady in the shallows, Themistokles called all the Athenian marines around him. He began his speech, 'All is at stake'; he urged them to die rather than live as slaves; the very future of the Greek people lay in their hands. As he finished, there was a dash for the galleys. Armeinias and his marines, wading waist-deep in the water, clambered aboard the trireme. At his signal, the three banks of rowers began to back-paddle into deep water, the helmsman dug in his port broad-oar and the prow swung round to head into the straits. The flute player set the beat and bending their backs to the task the oarsmen gently propelled the galley into line. As they turned line abreast to face the mouth of the straits, Armeinias found his trireme in the centre of the Athenian squadron.

Dawn broke and, '. . . the fair, white horses of the day came over all the land, lovely to see . . .', there lay the mighty Persian fleet, just a mile away. The jaded crews had been paddling all night, their look-outs constantly peering into the darkness for the escaping Greeks. The Persian admirals had become suspicious long before dawn, but the all-powerful Xerxes had given his orders, all they could do was obey. Ariabignes, the High Admiral and brother of the King, gave the order to attack. The sea foamed round the galleys as the blades of the oars dug deep; they leapt forward, the beat was raised, they were soon cutting swiftly through the water.

Then in 483/2 BC Themistokles introduced his Navy Bill, which turned Athens into a maritime state, establishing the sea-power which was the foundation of her empire. A rich, but unexpected silver lode had been struck in the state-owned mine at Laurium, worth 600,000 drachmas (1 drachma a day was a middle-class income, 200 the standard ransom for a man-at-arms). After state running costs, the surplus was to be divided among the citizens at a flat rate of 10 drachmas each. Themistokles persuaded the Assembly to use this surplus to provide a navy instead, enabling a ship-building programme to go ahead. Although the timber needed for the programme denuded Attica of trees and led to soil erosion, by the time of Salamis, Athens had built and equipped 200 triremes to replace her 70 outdated pentekonters. Naval training began in earnest, the rowers practising manoeuvring into line ahead and line abreast and 'breaking through' the enemy, the marines in handling their arms on a moving deck. By September, 480 BC, Athens had an efficient fighting navy, most effective in narrow waters, as their seamanship did not measure up to that of the Phoenicians, the mainstay of the Persian fleet.

The trireme used at Salamis (a translation from the Greek is 'three-fitted') appeared somewhere between 550 BC and 525 BC. It created a revolution in warship design, making all previous designs obsolete – much as the *Dreadnought*, 'all-big-gun' battleship made other ironclads obsolete at the turn of the twentieth-century. Although the trireme is surrounded by mystery, more so than any other warship in history, certain facts have emerged from writings, sculptured reliefs and drawings on urns and vases. Athenian naval records give the length of the oars to be between 13 feet 2 inches and 13 feet 10 inches. Ship sheds, excavated at Piraeus point to a maximum dimension of 110 feet in length, with a 10 feet beam.

The early triremes had a crew of 200, made up of 150 oarsmen in three banks, 50 oars in each bank; this left 50 officers, petty officers (helmsmen, look-out men, boatswains etc.) marines

and archers. By 480 BC the number of oarsmen had been increased to 170. The lowest level, the 'thralamite', had 27 oarsmen on each side, rowing through ports. They were close to the water, but high enough to allow a small boat to manoeuvre beneath them. One chronicle describes the use of small boats, rowing under the lower bank of oars, as a method of attack on triremes. The 'zugite', or second bank, also had 27 oarsmen each side. The top bank, the 'thranite', rowed through an outrigger which stretched some way beyond the ship's bulwark, to give greater

leverage, had 31 oarsmen each side. However, there is evidence that 30 extra oars were added at the bow and stern, bringing the total number of oarsmen up to 200. The fact that the blades of three oars, at different levels, operated in roughly a square yard of water, called for great rowing skill. But the Athenians were a skilful people and the ability of their oarsmen rapidly became the despair of their rivals at sea.

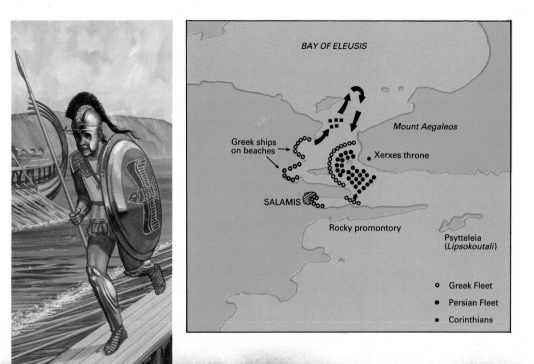

BELOW AND RIGHT: 'Armeinias ran towards the prow's bulwark as the bronze ram of the trireme bit deep into the Phoenician galley with a rending crash.'

The sound of singing drifted across the water; the Greeks were rhythmically chanting the awful Paian – 'O Saving Lord' – their battle hymn. Trumpets began to blare along the Greek lines. This was no fleeing enemy, the Greeks meant to stand and fight.

Xerxes, seated on a throne set up on a promontory at the foot of Mount Aegaleos, was surrounded by secretaries, taking note of each Persian commander's prowess. They would fight well watched by the King, their very lives depended on it. Both sides fought under oars, demasted; there was no room in the narrow straits for manoeuvring by sail. Both had a crew of about 200 to each ship, but the ships themselves, however, were designed for different tactics. The Persians, higher out of the water with towering sterns, relied on archers and javelin throwers to rain down missiles on the enemy, prior to boarding. For this reason they carried many more marines than the Greeks, and were faster through the water. The Greeks, on the other hand, had only 10 marines and 4 archers, aiming to ram and sink their opponents. Greek ships were heavier and flatter in the water, their bronze-headed rams an extension of the keel. More manoeuvrable under oars, they were also much steadier in a choppy sea.

Armeinias was at first dismayed when Eurybiades, the Greek Lord High Admiral, gave the order to back-paddle – but his own admiral, Themistokles, accepted the order quite cheerfully. The whole of the Athenian centre began to pull back, forming a crescent, drawing the Persian fleet towards the narrowest part of the channel. The Phoenicians, shortening their line, crammed between the island of Psyttaleia and Peiraieus, the Ionian squadron between the island and the rock promontory below Salamis town.

At the same time the daily wind blew up from the south, bringing with it a heavy swell and broken water, which made it difficult for the cramped Phoenician ships to keep a safe station. (The same south wind filled the sails of the 50 ships of Corinth as they scudded north to face the Egyptians. Although, after the battle an ugly rumour spread among the Athenians. It was whispered that the Corinthian Admiral, Adeimantos, panicked, hoisted sail and fled, followed by the rest of his squadron.)

Above the shouts and screamed insults of the Phoenicians, there was heard a great cry, echoing down the Greek line – 'Men, how much further are you going to back-water?' Many of the Greeks afterwards swore that it came from an 'apparition of a woman'; a few Athenians claimed to have seen their goddess, Pallas Athene. The trumpets blasted out, the Greek rowers dipped their oars, the triremes leapt forward. The astonished Phoenicians, their front line now only a few ships abreast, found themselves caught in a pincer movement, driven to the centre of the

channel, with no room to make use of their superior seamanship. The 30 ships of Aegina turned their rams towards the Ionian squadron.

The trireme of Armeinias got off to a racing start; he had always considered his oarsmen the best in the fleet, now they would prove it. Their blades churning the sea, they flew forward through a blanket of spray, the flute player raising the stroke until they were making over 12 knots. Pausing only to order the helmsman to steer to port, he ran to the prow to be among his marines. Already they were showing the rest of the fleet a clean pair of heels, they would be first into the attack. Armeinias clung to the prow's bulwark as a Phoenician galley loomed above them, broadside on. With a rending crash the bronze ram bit deep into the enemy below the water line; splinters flew as oars shattered; rowers were hurled from their benches. Bitter hand to hand fighting with javelin, lance and sword broke out at the prow. The Greek rowers frantically back-paddled, but the trireme was firmly wedged in the enemy. Now other Greek galleys were coming up in support.

At last Armeinias's trireme, breaking free, backed off, leaving a gaping hole in the side of the Phoenician – she began to heel over and sink, as water rushed into the rowing decks.

Marines and rowers alike flung themselves overboard to escape going down with the ship, but there was to be no escape. Small boats, launched from Salamis, manned by shore defence details, were, 'Clearing up the battlefield', clubbing the survivors to death as they struggled helplessly in the sea – '. . . as men gaff tunnies or some shoal of fish.' The sea reddened with blood as the Athenians exacted terrible revenge for the sacking of their city.

As the Phoenician front rows stopped, locked in combat, disabled or sinking, their following ships pressed on, adding to the confusion. They rammed each other in a desperate attempt to manoeuvre clear, littering the water with splintered oars and wreckage. By late afternoon, most of the enemy were in flight back to their base at Phalerum. Armeinias and his men, who had fought throughout the day, were tired but elated, there could be no doubt that the Greeks had won a famous victory. A group of enemy stragglers were still giving battle; Armeinias, calling for one final effort from his rowers, prepared to charge the nearest. To his amazement his intended victim rammed one of the other ships in the group and made off. Supposing the galley to be an enemy who had changed sides, he allowed her to pass. Later, after the battle, he learned to his chagrin that he had lost 10,000 drachmas, the reward for capturing Artmesia, Amazon Queen of Caria. Xerxes and his watchers were also deceived, believing she had sunk an Athenian ship, the King bitterly remarked – 'My men have

become women and my women men'. A group of Phoenician captains who had lost their ships, were not so lucky. They approached Xerxes, complaining that the Ionian squadron had given them no support, unfortunately for them the King had witnessed the bravery of the East Greeks, who were still fighting. Furiously he turned on the Phoenicians, ordering them to be beheaded – '. . . to put an end to their playing the coward themselves then blaming their betters.' Meanwhile the Persians on Psyttaleia had been cut to pieces by a force of Athenian hoplites ferried over from Salamis.

As darkness fell, the Greeks slowly paddled back to their beaches above Salamis town, singing songs of victory. The next morning they set out to attack the Persian fleet at Phalerum, but the enemy had gone, ordered by Xerxes to withdraw to Asia.

It had been a great victory, some said that 200 Persian ships had been destroyed or sunk and many more captured – the Greeks had lost 40 ships. Armeinias was one of two Athenians decorated for distinguished service.

Romans to the fifteenth century

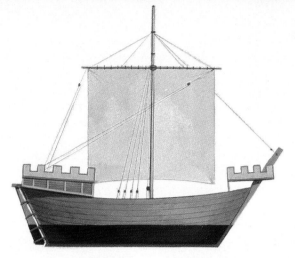

The Romans
The naval supremacy gained by the Greeks at Salamis could not save them from the invincible Roman legions sweeping eastwards across the Mediterranean, and they were eventually conquered. Although not themselves a seafaring people, the Romans were quick to learn from the skilful Greek shipwrights and craftsmen, and soon began to build their own fleets. By 260 BC, they were masters of the western Mediterranean, and following the Battle of Actium, off the north coast of Greece in 31 BC, they were able to dominate the whole of the Mediterranean area for the next 250 years.

The Romans were soldiers at sea rather than sailors, much as the Spaniards were in later days. For long-distance fighting, they fitted their ships with slings and heavy catapults for hurling missiles at the enemy; but they were much happier to come alongside, board and make the most of their short swords and throwing spears.
As time went on, the ships in the Mediterranean became bigger and bigger. King Ptolemy of Egypt, about the year 150 BC, was said to have had a galley 420 feet long, rowed by 4,000 oarsmen, with a crew of 2,800 mariners and soldiers.

The Vikings
The Mediterranean galleys with banks of rowers were totally unsuitable for the rougher seas of the north, here the people developed an entirely different type of vessel. A vessel designed to withstand the furious winter winds, mountainous waves and racing tides of the northern seas.

Originally the Vikings were men of the Viks, or bays, but before long the term came to mean a Norse sea-rover. The Viking ships built in Scandinavia from the eighth-century onwards, were double-ended vessels, low in the water, but sweeping upwards into high bows and sterns, often with an animal or dragon head at the prow. They were sturdy craft that behaved well in rough weather and many present day experts regard them as the most seaworthy sailing vessels ever evolved. Clinker-built (overlapping planks, each rivetted to the one below) of oak, they

were steered by a single oar placed on the right-hand side of the stern – the 'steerboard' or starboard side.

They carried a large, square sail and in the case of the fighting ships, the 'drakkar' or 'skeid', a single bank of oars, worked through circular ports cut in the gunwhale; the oarsmen, two to an oar, rowed standing up. The oar-ports could be sealed with deadlights when under sail alone, while the rowers were protected by a line of coloured wooden shields. The longships varied in size from smaller coastal vessels, usually 'sextensesse' (sixteen oars aside), to large fighting and sea-going craft. Most ships of the period had twenty oars aside, the 'Tyvesser' – although the 'Long Serpent' of King Olaf Tryggvason of Norway had thirty and King Canute's 'Great Dragon' as many as sixty, manned by 120 oarsmen. This craft, the biggest longship known in history, was 300 feet

The Fourteenth-century Cog
The cog, which appeared during the fourteenth-century, was a strong, but clumsy, single-masted ship completely decked in. By now the steering oar had been replaced by a central rudder and the fighting castles had become a permanent part of the ship. 90 feet in length, with a 10 feet draught, it was 24 feet in the beam and weighed 250 tons. The cog could be used either as a merchantman or fighting ship.

The Action off South Foreland, 1217
On August 24, 1217, an English fleet sailed from Dover to intercept a French squadron from Calais under the command of Eustace the Monk, a sea-rover in the pay of France. The English commander, Hugh de Burgh – Governor of Dover Castle and Commander of the narrow seas – who had with him 16 big ships and 20 smaller ones, introduced naval tactics for the first time. Making as if to attack Calais in their absence, he got the weather gage of the French, swung about and came up on their quarter. Whilst his bowmen fired down on the enemy from castle and fighting top, the

seamen made fast the ships with grapnels. Having the wind behind them, the English threw handfuls of unslaked powdered lime into the air, which was carried into the eyes of the Frenchmen, blinding them. Parties of seamen cut away rigging and halyards and in the confusion that followed, began a fearful slaughter of the blinded enemy.

Although the majority of the French fleet was able to beat back for Calais, a number of ships were towed to Dover as prizes. Eustace the Monk, found hiding in the hold of one of the ships, was dragged on deck and despite his pleas and promises of large rewards, was beheaded on the spot.

long and had a complement of around one thousand.

From 789 AD onwards, in ships such as these, the Vikings swept down from the north, plundering and colonising many parts of Britain and the Continent. Passing through the Columns of Hercules, they marauded their way across the Mediterranean as far as Con-

stantinople. Fearless, but ruthless, they spread terror wherever they went – 'From the Fury of the Norsemen Good Lord deliver us' – was a constant prayer throughout the Christian world, and part of the Litany.

LEFT: The Battle of Lepanto. The galleasse was a large galley, decked both for strength and convenience, which carried guns on its broadsides among the rowers, the first cannon to fire through gun ports. The inconvenience of having less rowers was compensated by three tall masts carrying lateen sails.

The Fifteenth-century Fighting ship

The end of the fourteenth and beginning of the fifteenth-century saw a considerable increase in the size of northern ships. Following the Viking tradition they were still clinker-built, but the fighting castles had become much larger and were an extension of the hull itself. Set high above the water, the now lofty forecastle made an ideal platform from which the bowmen could let fly their arrows and crossbow bolts into the waist of the enemy ship. By now the 'lateen' sail had been introduced, carried on a small mast at the stern – this enabled the helmsman to steer a truer course.

Ships were also being purpose built solely for fighting, no longer did they have to double up as merchantmen or troop transports. It was during this period that one of the most important turning points in naval history took place – the use of cannon at sea. The *Holigost* of Henry V, a ship of 760 tons, built in 1414, the most heavily-armed ship in the British Navy, carried only six pieces. By the end of the century, however, the cannon had taken firm hold and *Regent* built in 1489 could boast no less than 285 serpentines. Serpentines, although not large (their shot weighed only a few pounds), were designed mainly as a defence against boarders – but they could also be very effective as 'murdering pieces'. Many of them were mounted in swivels on the bulwarks and on the rails of the forecastle and quarterdeck, in order to sweep the waist of the ship, should the enemy gain a foothold in it.

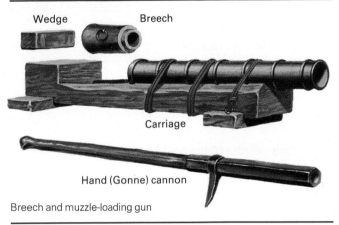

Wedge   Breech

Carriage

Hand (Gonne) cannon

Breech and muzzle-loading gun

The *Henry Grâce à Dieu*, 1514

Henry VIII's most famous fighting ship, *Henry Grâce à Dieu*, or 'Great Harry', was built in 1514 to meet the growing threat of Spain. The most advanced warship of her time, this towering four-master displaced over one thousand tons.

She was rebuilt between 1536 and 1539, when two rows of gun ports were cut into her hull to house 21 muzzle-loading bronze cannon, too heavy to be mounted high in the castles. She also mounted 122 medium-sized iron-cast guns, primitive breech-loaders.

The Battle of Lepanto, 1571

At first light on October 7, 1571, the look-outs in the leading galleasses of the Christian fleet sighted the Turkish sails, bearing down on them before a gusty wind. The fleet of the Holy Alliance, under the command of 25-year old, Don Juan of Austria, natural son of the Emperor Charles V, was made up of 285 galleys and galleasses and carried 29,000 men. The Holy Alliance, formed to crush the Turkish menace at sea, consisted of ships from Spain, Venice, Genoa, Malta and the Papal States. The Turkish fleet, which had been marauding in the Eastern Mediterranean, under the command of Ali Pasha, had 352 sail and carried 25,000 men.

As the two fleets approached each other in the Bay of Lepanto (**top left**) (now the Bay of Corinth) the wind suddenly dropped; oars became the sole motive power for both sides. The leading galleasses of the Christian fleet opened fire at about noon. The Turks had nothing to match them and were at first thrown into hopeless confusion, but they pressed forward and the battle became long and bloody. By the end of the day the Turks had been routed with the loss of practically all their commanders – Ali Pasha was beheaded – 190 of their ships had been captured and 20,000 of their men killed. 12,000 slaves, forced to serve in Ali Pasha's fleet were set free.

The *Henry Grâce à Dieu*, the 'Great Harry', the pride of Henry VIII's navy, was to become obsolete with the advent of Matthew Baker's designs.

John Kidde, Gunner on *Revenge,* 1588

BY THE guttering light of a tallow candle, John Kidde, gunner aboard *Revenge*, sat gnawing his hard tack and bit of dried fish. As he picked the weavils from the ship's biscuit he thought of that day the other side of the world, when poor old Ned Bright, long since dead, had lost four teeth biting into one. Ned's gums had been rotten with scurvy.

Rumour had been rife when John had joined *Pelican*, Francis Drake's flagship, back in 1577. Even John Wynter, captain of the Navy's *Elizabeth* and Vice-Admiral of the fleet, had sailed into Plymouth under the belief that he was joining an expedition to explore 'Terra Australis', that legendary continent in the Antarctic. The 153 other mariners who had signed on with John Kidde, were convinced that they were bound for Alexandria to take on a cargo of currants. How wrong they had all been!

From 20 October the crews had loaded ship under the eagle eye of the Admiral. One by one the casks of salt pork, ship's biscuit, flour, beer, peas, beans, lentils, onions and vinegar had been stowed away below; alongside the wine, water, dried fish and fresh cheeses. The Admiral had a nose for an over-ripe cheese and heaven defend any ship's victualler who tried to fob him off with a mouldy one. Spare canvas and spars were lashed down beside the pens for the hens and pigs. Harpoons, fish hooks and nets, to help supplement the rations with a supply of fresh fish, were carried aboard. The crew by tradition, grumbled. Plymouth wiseacres, loafing on the quayside, were intrigued by the armament going aboard – 18 demi-culverin for *Pelican* alone; such a vast number of cannon balls, so much gun powder – then bows, arquebuses, calivers and part-armour, enough for all 164 men aboard. A forge and blacksmith's tools? This was surely no expedition to pick up a load of currants from Egypt.

At last, on 13 December, 1577, after a storm-devastated false start, they had set sail, steering a south-westerly course. *Pelican*, flagship, length 100 feet, displacing 100 tons – *Elizabeth*, 80 tons – *Swan*, 50 tons – *Marigold*, 30 tons and a 15 ton bark, *Christopher*. Even before sailing there had been a growing resentment on the part of the crews towards the 10 'gentlemen adventurers' who had bought their way into the venture. The sons of landed families, they covered their ignorance of the sea by treating the common sailors with insolence and disdain.

Doubts felt when the ships passed the entrance to the Mediterranean, hardened when they turned west-

wards into the Atlantic. The fleet became a hive of buzzing rumour. Could they be heading for the New World? Was the Admiral leading them on another piratical sortie to plunder Spanish gold on the Main? They headed south-west by south into the Torrid Zone, the Doldrums – the Devil's Sea. Neither Admiral nor crews had ventured there before; Drake, a stern Protestant, could trust only in God and his own seamanship to see that his tiny ships limped through the humid, deathly still Doldrums before all his meat became rotten, his water foul. The old hands told awesome tales of sea monsters, demons and ghost ships; of seamen lured to a piteous fate. Tempers ran short, brawls began to flare up; discontent grew to the point of mutiny. John Brewer, Drake's trumpeter, reported to him that Thomas Doughty, captain of the newly-captured *Mary* and most influential of the gentlemen adventurers, was urging the men to mutiny and turn back for home. But Francis Drake was a cool one for sure, he had stayed his hand until the fleet, having made landfall in Brazil, headed down the South

Ships of the period were a hotbed of disease and infection, brought on by damp quarters and a lack of proper sanitation or hygiene. Before *Revenge* left Plymouth, wet broom twigs were burnt throughout the lower decks to fumigate them.

In theory everyone on board was paid at the same rate, ten shillings a month; but the allowances received by officers raised their pay to well above that of the lower deck. Prize money, divided at the discre- tion of the authorities was generally derisory. When the *Madre de Dios* was taken in 1592, Queen Elizabeth proposed that each seaman should receive twenty shillings as his share of a prize worth several hundreds of thousands of pounds. In the event, nearly every seaman went ashore with a pocketful of gems; diamonds, rubies, emeralds and pearls – nearly four-fifths of the treasure disappeared in this way.

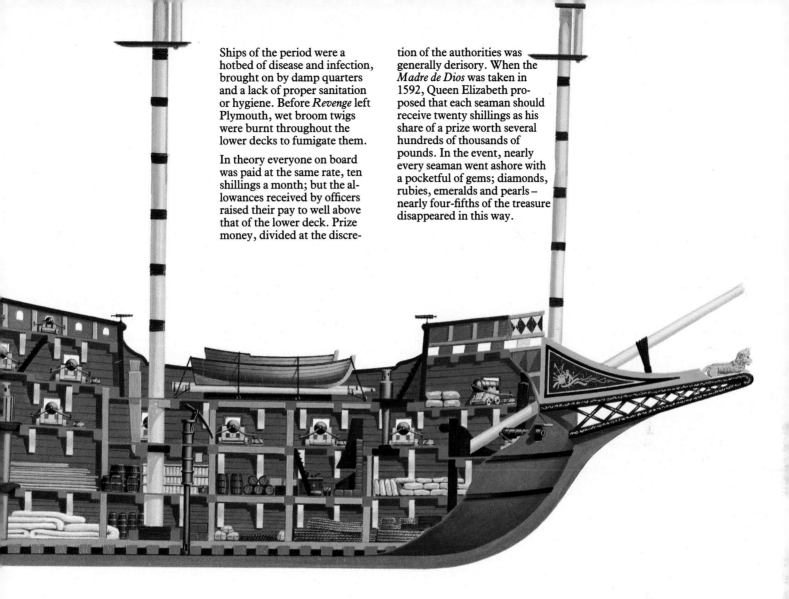

Revenge: a greyhound of a ship, low in the water like a galleasse, its length three times its beam.

American coast to St. Julian's Bay. There he held a court martial. Condemned unanimously by a jury of forty men selected from all five crews, Thomas Doughty was sentenced to be executed for inciting mutiny. Two days later, 2 June 1578, he was led out to the block on an island in the bay, to be beheaded – after taking communion and sharing dinner with Drake. His last words were to the executioner, 'Strike clean and with care, for I have a short neck.'

There was no more talk of mutiny after that!

The crews named the island – the Island of Blood.

A few days later Francis Drake called them together ashore and told them they were going through the Magellan Straights into the Pacific Ocean. No one was bold enough to question the Admiral. Looting and plundering, claiming lands in the name of the Queen, 'El Draco' had made his way across the Pacific and

Whilst at sea, sailors of the period were allowed 8¼d (1d is the rough equivalent of ½p) for victuals on a 'flesh (meat) day' and only 4¾d on a 'fish' day.

Flesh days Tuesday, Thursday, Saturday and Sunday.

Biscuit (hard tack)	1lb	1d
Beer	1 gallon	1¾d
Salt beef or pork	2lbs	5½d
		8¼d

Fish or Banyan days Monday, Wednesday, Friday.

Biscuit (hard tack)	1lb	1d
Beer	1 gallon	1¾d
Butter	¼lb	½d
Cheese	¼lb	½d
Stockfish	½ a fish	1d
		4¾d

To this was added salt, water, vinegar and on rare occasions, wine. At first glance this appears to be reasonable, but it must be remembered that the butter was often as not rancid when it came aboard; the meat half putrid and the biscuit, weavil-ridden. After a month at sea rations were all but uneatable. On long voyages six men had to subsist on the usual rations for four.

Punishment

Punishment aboard Elizabethan ships was both swift and brutal – designed to fit the crime. Later, in Nelson's time, all offences would be punished by either flogging or hanging. A Tudor captain, all-powerful, meted out rough justice – his word was final. Should a sailor draw a weapon on officer or messmate to cause, 'tumult and likelihood of murther or bloodshed', his right hand would be struck off before the assembled ship's company. A thief, the crime proven, was ducked three times from the bowsprit, each time being dragged clear on the point of drowning. On nearing land he would be towed ashore from a boat's stern, given a loaf of bread and 'banished their Grace's ships for ever'. Murderers were bound hand and foot to their victims and flung overboard.

Anyone caught drunk aboard ship, spent time in the bilboes (nautical stocks). Confirmed drunkards had heavy iron weights attached to their arms and slung from their necks to increase the pain.

Mutineers and would-be mutineers were drummed to the yard arm and hanged – gentlemen beheaded.

For anyone endangering the ship or the lives of his shipmates by falling asleep on watch, the punishment was cruel, and at the same time curious. The offender was given three chances to mend his ways. At the first offence he was lashed to the main mast with a bucket of water on his head. The second time he was hung up by the wrists and two buckets of water poured into his sleeves. Taken asleep the third time, the culprit was 'bound to the Mast with Platts and certain gun chambers tyd to his Arms and Thighs; much pain to his Body at the will of the Capt.' This was his final chance; should he be caught asleep again, he was hung from the bowsprit, with a 'Can of Beer and a loaf of Bread' – his choice – 'to hang there till he starved or cut himself into the sea'.

Indian Oceans. In an attempt to placate Sir Christopher Hatton, whose secretary, Thomas Doughty, he had executed, Drake renamed his flagship 'Golden Hind', which was the badge of Hatton, captain of the Queen's guard, and one of her favourites. Drake finally dropped anchor in Plymouth Sound on Monday, 26 September, 1580. The Queen, although publicly denouncing Drake, had privately 'dubbed' him 'Sir' Francis Drake, who in terms of to-day, had brought back loot to the value of £25,000,000. John Kidde chuckled over the bag of Spanish doubloons that had been his share – long since frittered away in the taverns of Plymouth. John swilled down another mouthful of biscuit and fish with a swig of beer. How well he remembered that voyage; the beer, made without hops, had long been sour and they had all suffered agonies of dysentery, except the Admiral and the gentlemen adventurers – they had had wine.

Propped against his 18 pounder culverin, he rolled easily with the movement of the ship as the 500 ton *Revenge* buffeted her way up the English Channel in pursuit of the Spanish Armada. The galleons, galleasses, galleys and carracks of Spain had appeared off the Scilly Isles 11 days before, 19 July, 1588 – 130 proud ships sailing in a tight crescent formation, the horns of the crescent to the stern. They were making for Plymouth in the hope of catching the English fleet napping. Old Tom Flemyng, captain of the bark *Golden Hind*, spotting them off the Lizard, had scurried into Plymouth, breathlessly breaking the news to the English admirals. All had been scamper. Galleons and merchantmen, warped from the Sound, were soon beating out to sea on the edge of a westerly wind. The Dons had the shock of their lives at first light; there, astern to port, bobbed the English fleet, 102 sail, lying to windward. But some did say that the Vice-Admiral, Sir Francis Drake, had stayed to finish a game of bowls.

The Spanish were scudding up the Channel before a brisk south-westerly wind, still in a tight crescent, led by four Neopolitan galleasses. 130 ships carrying 8,000 sailors, 2,000 rowers, 19,000 soldiers and 1,500 volunteers and non-combatants. Among the latter were 180 friars; the Spanish sailors – notoriously superstitious – regarded them with growing horror, everyone knew that it was unlucky to have priests aboard ship. The Armada made an impressive sight; its towers and yards festooned with hundreds of multi-coloured flags and pennants streaming in the wind; its billowing sails gaudy with painted crosses and holy pictures. The friars, scattered amongst the ships, exhorted nobleman and peasant alike to be steadfast and valiant in the Holy Cause, Philip II's 'Enterprise against England' – there was to be stern suppression of blasphemy. The King's orders to the Admiral, the Duke of Medina Sidonia, were clear and to the point.

A contemporary artist's impression of the Armada at the Lizard

He was to link up with the Duke of Parma's army in the Netherlands for a joint invasion of England – avoiding naval action unless it was forced upon him. Now here were the English, buzzing about him like a swarm of angry wasps.

When the English Admiral, Lord Howard of Effingham, ordered the attack, *Revenge*, flying Drake's flag, longer and lower in the water, far more manoeuvrable, had flitted round the more cumbersome Spaniards pouring in a broadside and scurrying off. The English fired their guns on the down-roll, aiming to send their shot smashing into the enemy's gun decks, the flying splinters creating havoc among the guns' crews. On the other hand, the Spaniards fired their cannon on the up-roll, in the hope of bringing down mast and yards, allowing them to go alongside and board the enemy. For this reason they carried far more soldiers than seamen, relying on hand to hand combat on ship deck rather than seamanship and gunnery.

On the cramped gun deck of *Revenge*, amidst the swirling smoke, the crash of leaping guns and the shouts and curses of the gunners, John worked his 18 pounder until it was hot. His gunner's mate rammed down a wet sponge to cool it, a cloud of steam rolled out of the barrel. Stripped to the waist, sweating from the effort, he and his crew fired salvo after salvo into the Spaniards. During a lull in the fighting, they swilled down drinking water from a cask; it was already becoming brackish and they only a day out of Plymouth – those ship's victuallers had a lot to answer for.

During the afternoon the Spanish galleon *San Salvador* blew up – it was said aboard *Revenge* that a German mercenary aboard, a gunner, having been severely flogged by the captain, lit a fuse to the powder magazine and jumped overboard. The flagship of the Andalusian squadron, *Nuestra Señora del Rosario*, commanded by Don Pedro de Valdes, colliding with another ship in the closely-packed formation, suffered the loss of her main mast. With night fast approaching in a rising sea, she was left to fend for herself. The Spanish Admiral had no intention of fighting a pitched battle, he would follow his orders to the letter and sail the Armada to Dunkirk to join the Duke of Parma in an invasion of England. Although out-sailed and out-gunned, the Duke's ships suffered little or no damage from the pounding broadsides poured into them by the English. Walls of oak were more than a match for the cannon shot of the period, unless fired at point-blank range. During the entire engagement neither side lost a single ship of any size through gunfire alone.

That night *Revenge* acted as a guide to the English fleet. The great poop lantern was lit as a beacon and the crew settled down to stalk the Spaniards, the remainder of the Fleet trustingly followed the guiding light. Suddenly the light had gone out, throwing them into confusion. In the face of later criticism, Drake maintained, that, seeing the vague shape of ships to seaward, he had doused the light and accompanied by the privateer, *Roebuck*, had turned away to investigate. Finding the ships to be a fleet of harmless German merchantmen, neutrals in the fight, he swung to port to take up with the Armada again. By now it was dawn and there, wallowing ahead of him, lay the crippled *Rosario*. Her commander promptly surrendered, thinking it no disgrace to give in without a fight to 'El Draco'. John Kidde heard two of the gentlemen whisper a different tale. Neither had seen any Germans, in fact no ships at all, and the Vice-Admiral had never been averse to a bit of piracy. Drake's proverbial luck had held good; *Rosario* proved to be the most valuable prize taken from the Armada. In her strong room were 55,000 gold ducats and Pedro de Valdes himself fetched a ransom of £3,000. For days the pursuit had gone on; an indecisive battle off the Isle of Wight had frustrated a landing, but the Armada, for the most part intact, still maintained a tight crescent, and forged on towards Dunkirk.

Yesterday, 27 July, Medina Sidonia had anchored his fleet in the Calais roads – the English lay-to, less than a culverin shot away. After dark, the gunner left his hammock – one of those new-fangled South American Indian 'hammacoes' brought back and popularised by Sir John Hawkins – and went to the upper deck to see a messmate who was standing an hour's regulation punishment. The puritanical ship's Master had overheard him blaspheme. 'A maudlin-spike (*viz.* an iron pin) clapt close into their mouths until they are very bloody; an excellent cure for swearers.' From the Great Cabin came the sound of music and laughter. At sea Drake lived in style, dining off silver plates edged with gold. Preserved fruits and other delicacies were washed down with the choicest wines, and ewers of perfumed water stood ready to rinse greasy fingers. John thought of the piece of dried fish and weavil-ridden biscuit that had served him for supper – still, the ale had been good.

To starboard, lit up like Christmas trees, the

Spanish galleons rode at anchor, the voices of their crews came clearly across the water. Sentimental Spanish songs accompanied by lutes. But these revelries were soon to be silenced. The Master came round calling for volunteers, Lord Howard had decided to send in fire-ships among the closely anchored Armada. Eight merchant ships were commandeered for the 'Firing of the Spanish Navy', the owners compensated for the loss of their ships to the tune of £5,111. Sir Francis Drake's share of this, for the loss of his ship, the 200 ton *Thomas*, was £1,000. Around midnight the fire-ships were towed into position by ships' boats; with sails set, guns loaded and rudders lashed, they were fired and allowed to drift with the tide and wind towards the massed Spanish ships. Crammed full of pitch, barrels of gunpowder and other combustibles, they slowly bore down on the Spaniards, spewing out flame and sulphurous smoke. They made an awesome

Scurvy

This disease was dreaded above all others by Elizabethan mariners, the cause of untold hardship and suffering during long voyages of exploration. Caused by a lack of Vitamin C, ascorbic acid, it played havoc with a ship's crew (Vitamin C was not isolated until 1928). Yet even in Elizabethan times experienced captains were aware that this deficiency disease could be prevented by including fresh fruit and vegetables in a crew's diet. As early as 1570, one old sea dog, Captain Lancaster, discovered that his ship's company did not suffer from scurvy if they were given daily doses of lime juice. By the end of the eighteenth-century this had become a compulsory part of a British tar's diet, earning him the nickname 'Limey'.

Captain Cook was one of the first navigators to tackle the problem of scurvy with conviction and determination; it was his proud boast that during his second voyage in the Pacific, lasting three years, he never lost a man through the disease. He insisted his men ate 'sour krout' (cabbage pickled in salt and juniper berries) and when they came across it, wild celery and scurvy grass. Anyone refusing these was punished – Cook's Journal tells of Able Seaman Harry Stephens and Thomas Dunster, private of Marines, each receiving twelve

lashes of the 'Cat' for refusing their rations.

Symptoms of scurvy
1. A growing listlessness, the slightest movement becomes too much effort. Victims still eat and drink well.
2. Roughness of the skin on upper arms and thighs – sometimes boils and spots – the complexion becomes yellow and bloated.
3. The gums swell, become painful and bleed, the teeth loosen in their sockets and frequently fall out.
4. Unbearable pain in joints on movement.
5. Black bruises under the skin.
6. The feet and legs may swell.
7. Sometimes a crackling noise in the bones is noticed. 'In some, though more rarely on each motion of their joints, a noise is heard as from broken bones, or like the cracking of nuts.'

Pains in the chest and laboured breathing is followed by a sudden and unexpected death.

Even when the disease has become far advanced it can be rapidly cured by food containing Vitamin C – blackcurrants, rose hips, strawberries, peppers, sprouts, lemon and lime juice.

Early remedies
Oil of vitriol (sulphuric acid), cider, vinegar, sea water and onions.

sight, enough to unsettle even the bravest seaman.

But Medina Sidonia, expecting fire-ships, had stationed pinnaces to drag them away from his fleet before they could do any damage. The first two were quickly caught and towed off to burn themselves out. But when the guns began to explode with the heat, their flying shot sent the pinnace crews into a panic and they allowed the other six through '. . . spurting fire, and their ordnance shooting, which was a horror to see' – as one witness put it. At a signal-gun fired from the Duke's flagship, a number of large galleons slipped their cables and made for the open sea, but the majority cut loose and scattered in confusion, colliding

LEFT: the Launch of the Fire-ships. '. . . *all in flames, burning furiously in the bows, with the mainsails and foresails set, and the rudders lashed.*' (Spanish eye-witness account).

with each other in their frantic attempt to reach clear water.

San Lorenzo, one of the mighty Neopolitan galleasses, was driven hard on to the Calais Beach by her panic-stricken rowers. She was immediately attacked by Lord Howard and taken. Hugo de Moncada, commander of the galleasses, was killed during the action, the only senior Spanish officer to fall in the 'Enterprise against England'. As dawn broke on 29 July, the ships of the Armada could be seen strung out along the French coast as far as Dunkirk, gone for ever was the disciplined crescent formation. It was every ship for herself as they were driven up the Channel by a blustery westerly wind, hotly pursued by the English.

Shafts of light from the open ports were flooding into the gun deck as John Kidde went up top to the fresh air; the air below after a sweltering night was rank with a dozen different smells. The Spanish fleet lay dead ahead making heavy weather of it, within the hour the English would be alongside. The ship's drummer, 'beating to quarters' on 'Drake's Drum' – already becoming a legend – sent the gunner scampering down to his culverin. But not before he had heard Sir Francis Drake's shout of glee – 'We have them

ABOVE: Guns played an all-important part in the Armada campaign.
A the Culverin, long range weapon favoured by the English;
B the heavy cannon, the Spanish preference, effective only at short range and, as such, instrumental in their defeat;
C a bronze rat-tailed breech-loading falconet on a two-truck carriage of a type used in ships and fortresses in the second half of the sixteenth century;

INSET: a seventeenth century English musketeer.

before us, and mind with the Grace of God to wrestle a fall with them.'

Craning through the gun port, John saw that Drake was steering for the Duke's squadron of five, still miraculously together. As they neared the stern of the Spanish flagship, the *San Martin*, her 300 soldiers lining the rails, took in sail and lay-to, swinging beam on to the English. The Duke of Medina Sidonia had decided to stand and fight. But Drake, followed by the rest of his squadron, swept past, pouring in broadside after broadside. No longer playing at 'long bowls', they were in 'half a musket shot' of the enemy. Their shot took frightful toll of the packed soldiery; smashed mast and rigging and ploughed into ships' sides. Remorselessly the Armada was driven towards the treacherous Zeeland sands, only a miracle could save it. It must have seemed just that to the priests, fervently praying on the poop decks. For, with less than five fathoms beneath the keels of the galleons, the wind swung round to the south-west sending the Armada scudding into the North Sea.

Helpless to turn, with many of the ships out of shot, the Armada swept north before the prevailing wind. The 'Enterprise against England' was over. A broken man, Medina Sidonia realising that his scattered and badly mauled fleet would never be able to join up with the Duke of Parma, put himself in the hands of God and returned to Spain round the north coast of Scotland. There was no more fighting – English powder rooms were empty – they had run out of round shot.

Only two Spanish ships were sunk in the battle, three were abandoned to the enemy, three ran ashore in France and two in Holland. Nineteen were wrecked off the rocky coasts of Scotland and Ireland – their crews invariably massacred. Thirty-five disappeared without trace, never to be accounted for. About half the Armada limped back to Spain with only a miserable fragment of their original crews. Philip II, bitterly disappointed, ascribed his defeat to the Will of God, writing – 'I sent my ships to fight against the English, not the wind and waves.' But really the defeat of the Armada showed the futility of sending soldiers to fight sailors at sea.

John Kidde and his messmates yarned, sprawled out on the gun deck; wounds, rotten food, harsh treatment and the stench of the ship forgotten – a hero's welcome awaited them at Plymouth.

Midshipman Roberts aboard *Victory* at Trafalgar, 1805

MIDSHIPMAN Richard Roberts braced himself against the slow roll of *Victory*'s quarterdeck as the flagship wallowed towards the combined French and Spanish fleets. HMS *Victory*, a First Rate displacing 2162 tons, carrying 104 guns, with a crew of 850, had first come into commission in the Royal Navy in 1778. Since then her flag had flown at a dozen engagements with the French and Spanish. A proud ship, with a proud crew, she was majestically leading the Battle Line into action.

HMS *Victory*: Lord Nelson's favourite flagship. Apart from the great cabin, the accommodation was cramped, the deckheads low.

The Guns on the *Victory*

Number	Weight of shot	Length of gun	Weight of gun	Normal charge of powder	Velocity	Diameter of shot	Point blank range	Extreme range	Penetration of shot		Type of shot
Lower Gun Deck 30	32 pr long	9' 6"	55 cwt 2 qrs	10 lb 11 ozs	1600' per sec	6.1" (6.41)	350 yds	2,900 yds	10.11 lbs charge	30" Elm	Round
Middle Gun Deck 28	24 pr long	9' 6"	50 cwt	8 lb	1600' per sec	5.5" (5.823)	248 yds	2,573 yds	16 lbs charge	45" Elm	Grape Case Chain
Upper Gun Deck Forecastle Quarter deck 44	12 pr long	9'	34 cwt	3½ lb (4 lbs)	1600' per sec	4.8" (4.623)	300 yds	1,800 yds	12 lb charge	41" Elm	Bar Langridge
Upper Deck 2	68 lb Caronades	5' 5"	35 cwt	5½ lbs	750' per sec	7.8" (8.05)	200 yds	1,280 yds			

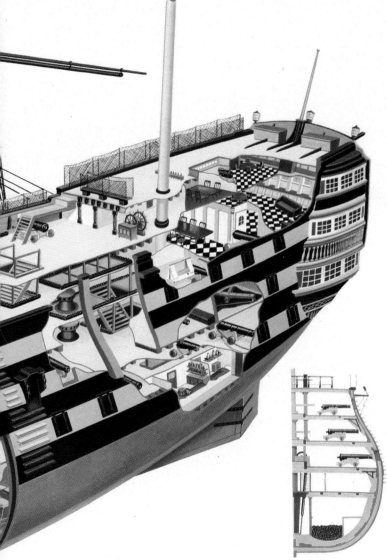

Statistics at Trafalgar

	Number of ships	Number of guns	Number killed	Number wounded	Ships lost
British	27	2,176	449	1,291	None
French	19	1,356	3,321	976	23
Spanish	15	1,270	1,047	1,397	
	34	2,626	4,368	2,373	

As Admiral's messenger, Richard had stationed himself beside the rear 12 pounder to be close to Lord Nelson, ready to leap forward at the slightest nod from the Commander in Chief of the British fleet. It was approaching noon on 21 October, 1805. He watched the gun's crew run out the 34 cwt 'Long' 12 pounder at the first roll of the marine's drum 'Beating to Quarters', until its wicked-looking nine foot barrel jutted well beyond the gun port. The captain of the gun, Gunner's Mate John Brown, already at 30 a veteran of several hot engagements with the French, attached his lanyard to the flint-lock on the gun breach. Thomas Twitchet, a cheeky twelve-year-old powder monkey and the youngest aboard *Victory*, staggered up from the hanging magazine four decks below – the orlop deck. He was loaded down with flannel bags, each filled with 3½ lbs of gunpowder, the charges that could, if necessary, propel the 12 lb shot for over a mile.

It had taken less than ten minutes from the drummer's tattoo for Victory to 'clear for action'. Decks had been sluiced down and strewn with sand to prevent men slipping in blood once the fighting became heavy. Each gun on the three gun decks had been provided with a dozen shot in rope bags, and half-pikes and cutlasses stood ready to hand for boarding and hand to hand fighting. From fore to aft the ship had been stripped; baggage and all but the most necessary furniture stowed away in the hold; stern windows removed, stern chaser guns run out. Below decks wet 'fearnought' screens had been rigged to reduce fire risk; buckets of water for fire-fighting and drinking were at hand, alongside piles of oranges for quenching smoke-parched throats. Splinter nets festooned the upper-decks, rigged to catch falling blocks and spars. Ship's boats were put over the side to be towed astern – they would be needed after the action, also, getting them off the deck lessened the risk of deadly flying splinters. Extra spars and tackle were stacked neatly on the weather deck. HMS *Victory* was ready to fight.

At 11.00 hours there had been a welcome issue of grog, but that was nearly an hour ago and now the British Weather Squadron was rolling through a heaving swell with barely enough wind to billow out their fully-set sails. Led by *Victory* they crawled at less than 3 knots towards the massed guns of the enemy, scarcely a mile ahead. A glance to starboard showed him that Vice-Admiral Collingwood's Leeward Squadron was already engaging the French.

Mouth dry, stomach knotted in sickening fear, Richard could feel the sweat trickling down his spine, icy cold beneath his canvas shirt despite the hot October sun. At 20, old for a midshipman (he had come up through the lower-deck), he had known fear before at Copenhagen, but never fear like this. They were sitting ducks as they sailed, oh so slowly, towards the Franco-Spanish 42 pounders. The Commander in Chief, Vice-Admiral Lord Nelson, paused in his

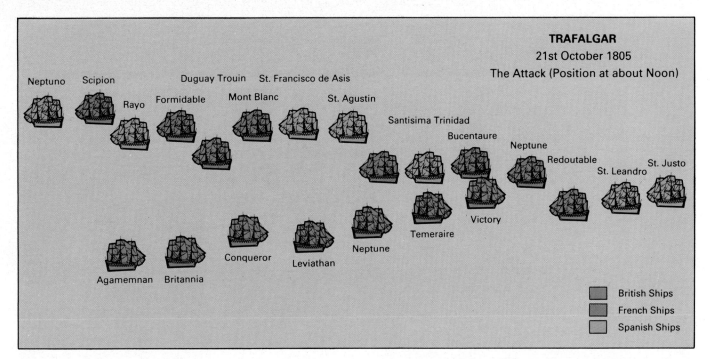

Neptuno Scipion Rayo Formidable Duguay Trouin St. Francisco de Asis Mont Blanc St. Agustin Santisima Trinidad Bucentaure Neptune Redoutable St. Leandro St. Justo Victory Temeraire Neptune Leviathan Conqueror Britannia Agamemnan

British Ships
French Ships
Spanish Ships

steady pacing of the quarterdeck and turned to his signal lieutenant, 'I'll now amuse the fleet with a signal. Mr. Pascoe, send, "England expects that every man will do his duty" '. Using Popham's telegraphic code the signal flags were run up the halyard. This was closely followed by signal number 16 – 'Engage the enemy more closely' – a signal that fluttered from the top-gallant mast-head until shot away. The unnatural quiet that had been hanging over *Victory* was broken; loud and repeated cheering rang throughout the ship, to be echoed along the Battle Line of the British fleet.

The enemy ran up their colours, the Spanish also mounting large wooden crosses at their mast-heads. Grinning, John Brown turned to Richard, 'They'll stop some shot, I shouldn't wonder.' Flame flickered along the sides of the French First Rates; through the smoke came the first ball, the range 800 yards – it dropped short. The second sent up a column of water alongside, drenching a gun's crew on the lower gun-deck. The third ball tore a gaping hole through one of the top sails. It was now 12.20 hours, Nelson had engaged the French and Spanish off Cape Trafalgar.

The work became hot as eight enemy ships blazed away at the British flagship. At 600 yards *Victory*'s mizen top-mast was shot away; a ball that came screaming through the rigging inches above Richard's head smashed the steering-wheel. 'Rig for steering by relieving tackles on the main-deck.' Outwardly calm and detached, Captain Hardy gave the order crisply. A man went screaming across the quarterdeck, a foot-long wooden splinter jutting from his stomach, two loblollies hurried him below to the surgeon's cockpit. Richard, eyes on the Admiral, saw Mr. Scott, Nelson's secretary, all but cut in two by a cannon ball – he died instantly. Severely battered, her hull scored with shot,

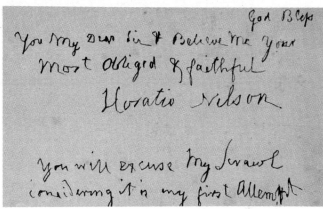

Nelson's first attempt to write with his left hand.

her spars shot away, *Victory* held her way in silence. Not a shot was fired in reply. Already 50 men lay dead or wounded as she made towards *Bucentaure*, flagship of Vice-Admiral Villeneuve, the Franco-Spanish Commander in Chief. Amidst flying splinters of mast and spar, the gun crews remained steady, waiting the order to fire. A double-headed shot scythed through a party of marines on the poop, killing eight and wounding others. 'This is too warm work, Hardy, to last long.' Nelson's words raised a laugh, the Admiral had a reputation for coolness among the lower-deck.

12.59 hours – *Bucentaure* loomed up on the port beam, they surely must ram her. Leaning over the side, Richard saw *Victory* brush the stern of the French flagship, her main yard-arm caught in the enemy's after rigging. The French ensign, drooping in the still air, was within arm's-reach of the upper-deck.

'Fire.'

Nelson mortally wounded at Trafalgar 21 October 1805, by D. Dighton.

As she swept slowly past, William Willmet, *Victory*'s Bo'sun (Boatswain) jerked his firing lanyard; the port forward carronade – the 'smasher' – roared out. Crammed with a 68 lb ball and a keg of 500 bullets, it fired straight into the after cabin windows of Villeneuve's flagship. One by one, *Victory*'s port broadside, 52 guns in all, some double-shotted, the rest treble-shotted, poured in cannon balls at point-blank range, as each gun in turn bore down on *Bucentaure*. Through the flame and smoke came the screams and cries of the stricken French. The first deadly broadside tore through the gun-decks dismounting twenty cannon and killing or wounding nearly 400 men, half the crew of *Bucentaure*.

'Port the helm, Mr. Atkinson.' The ship's Master hurried below to carry out Captain Hardy's order – he obviously intended to run aboard *Redoutable*, now blasting away at the British flagship. As *Victory*'s head swung to port, Richard could see the crew of the French ship scampering on to her upper-decks ready to board. The enemy's lower-deck ports slammed shut, *Redoutable*'s captain had no intention of allowing the British to board him through them. A splintering crash as the yards of the two ships smashed into each other sent him grabbing for the rigging – a musket ball ricochetted from the barrel of the 12 pounder – they were alongside the Frenchman. It was 13.10 hours. Locked together the ships hammered each other with point-blank broadsides. *Victory*'s starboard 'smasher' swept the crowded decks of the French '74' with a murderous fire, the starboard broadside raked her from stem to stern. The muzzles of their guns actually touching the enemy, they continued to pour shot into the lowered gun-ports of *Redoutable*. Richard, stumbling with a message through the dense smoke and clamour of the lower gun-deck, was astonished to see the firemen of the 32 pounders dashing water into the holes drilled into the enemy after each shot. Lieutenant Yule put him right – 'If they catch fire, so will we.'

Glad to be once more on the upper-deck away from the shambles below, the midshipman was horrified to find himself caught in a fierce hail of musket fire and hand grenades from the *Redoutable*'s tops. Captain Lucas had trained his 'people' well in musketry, they

Gunnery on the *Victory*

The sight that greeted Richard Roberts when he reached the lower gun deck at the height of the action was unbelievable. He never ceased to wonder how the gunners handling the heavy 32 pounders could remain sane – many did not and nearly all suffered from bad hearing. To reach the heavy guns he had to pass through the upper gun deck with its battery of thirty 12 pounders; then through the middle gun deck where twenty-eight 24 pounders were blazing off, down to the lower gun deck.

Dimly-lit by single-candle battle lanthorns swinging from the deckhead, it was a hell of noise, smoke and seemingly – chaos. Choking gunpowder fumes set him coughing and he could scarcely see across the 50 feet wide deck for swirling smoke which totally obscured the best part of its 150 feet length. It was hideous with noise; the crash of firing cannon, the thump as leaping guns hit the deck on recoil, the hurraying at a hit; shouts, curses, groans; the clatter of ropes and the grumbling of blocks. Deftly making his way past black-faced gunners, across a deck slippery with blood, he paused by a 32 pounder. The captain of the gun, slow, easy-going William Brown, an old hand of 45, was now a shouting tyrant bullying his 15 man gun crew to greater

efforts. A tall man, his head brushed the low deckhead, he took a pride in his shooting, drilling his crew into a highly disciplined team. As a result they handled their gun with clockwork precision. Richard, half blinded by the flash and deafened by the blast as the cannon fired, was aware of the gun leaping back until the muzzle was some 3 feet clear of the gun port; at this point the breech rope took the strain and killed the recoil. Rapidly the train tackle attached to the rear of the gun carriage was fixed to a ring bolt and hauled taught to hold it steady against the roll of the ship. With split second timing a hand jumped forward, pushed a reamer down the muzzle then dragged it out, scattering smouldering frag-

ments of the previous charge. In went the wet sponge to clean and cool the barrel; the flannel bag of gunpowder was snatched from the powder monkey and rammed down the barrel into the breech. This was followed by the wad, then the 32 lb round shot, another wad and rammed hard home. The second wad prevented a gap developing between the charge and shot as the ship rolled – a gap would burst the gun on firing.
Meanwhile, the gun's captain had jabbed an iron 'pricker' down the touch hole or vent, piercing the flannel bag of gunpowder and pushed in a quill snatched from his pouch (the quill, containing powder in spirit of wine, helped the flash through from the flint-lock to

the charge). A quick sprinkle of loose powder from his powder horn into the pan of the flint-lock and the gun was being run out, by the crew easing the train tackle and heaving on the side tackles. William Brown cocked the flint-lock, sighted along the barrel and jerked his firing lanyard. The flash travelled down the quill, the gun roared and was leaping back again. The whole operation had taken just 90 seconds.

The rate of fire of such disci-plined crews, coupled with the speed of a flint-lock over a slow-burning match, was to prove a major factor in securing such a decisive victory at Trafalgar. The French crews took twice as long to fire off a round, the Spanish even longer.

---

were now systematically picking off any English seaman who broke cover on *Victory*'s upper-deck. A deadly stream of langridge from the brass cohorns positioned in the fore and main tops, wrought havoc among *Victory*'s upper-deck gunners, almost silencing the 12 pounders.

A few feet away, the Admiral still pacing the quarterdeck, suddenly staggered and fell on his face. Nelson had been hit. A musket ball from a French soldier perched in the mizen-top, 15 yards above, had passed through his left epaulette, driven down through his lung and lodged in his spine. A word from Hardy, who had pleaded with Nelson not to wear all his decorations – in vain – and Sergeant Secker, marine, and two seamen lifted the Admiral and carried him below. Although in great pain Nelson covered his face with a handkerchief, lest the 'people' see he had been wounded. Gently they laid him on the purser's bed, where William Beatty, ship's surgeon examined

him – he looked up with tears in his eyes and sadly shook his head. It was 13.25 hours. Midshipman Roberts never saw the Commander-in-Chief again.

But Richard had his own worries.

Joseph Ward, Ordinary Seaman, 20 and popular, fell against him, shot through the head. Boy 2nd Class, George Wilson, powder monkey, 15, fell shrieking to the deck, shot through the back. Young Thomas Whimple, already at 18 a captain's clerk, also lay dead, not a mark on him – his breath drawn out by the wind of a round shot. Richard's messmate, Bill Rivers, midshipman, clung whimpering to the side rigging, his left shin shattered.

Crouching behind the 12 pounder, he gazed about him with horror, nearly everyone on the flagship's upper-deck had either been killed or wounded by the French riflemen in her mizen-tops. The success of his riflemen in clearing *Victory*'s upper-deck, encouraged Captain Lucas to make one final attempt to take the

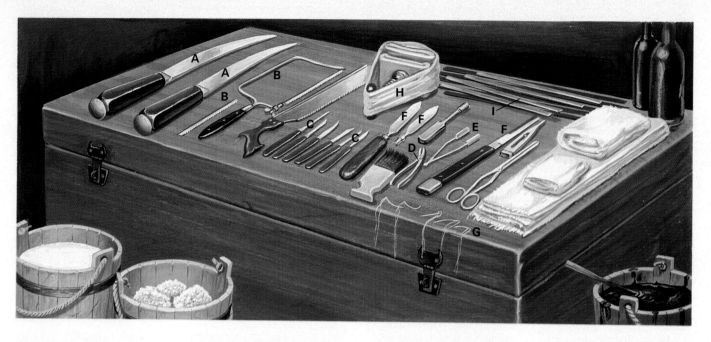

Surgery at sea

At 'Beat to Quarters', there was feverish activity in the surgeon's cockpit on the orlop deck. Dr. William Beatty, the *Victory*'s surgeon, had a space cleared to receive the wounded once the enemy ships were engaged. The midshipmans' chests were dragged across the red-painted deck to form a platform covered with a folded sail on which to lay out the wounded (treatment was carried out in strict rotation; first down, first treated, whether officer or rating). Little notice would be paid to the type of wound, in consequence many would die through loss of blood who might well have been saved. These chests would be used as an operating table, although too low for comfortable surgery, which might go on for hours. In rough weather Dr. Beatty would lash himself to a stanchion while he operated. At each end of the 'operating table' were placed two smoking candles, the only light in the dim cockpit, apart from two or three horn lanterns on the bulkheads.

The instruments were neatly laid out on another chest;
A two amputating knives,
B one amputating saw with a spare blade, **C** six scalpels,
D a pair of bullet forceps and a **E** bullet stoop, **F** two catlins (double-edged amputating knives), **G** crooked needles of all sizes (already threaded,
H tourniquets to stop the flow of blood (Petit's screw tourniquet allowed the patient to op-

erate it himself) and **I** wooden and iron splints for fractures. There was a large quantity of scraped lint, some mixed with flour in a bowl; bandages of all lengths and breadths, dry swabs for mopping up the blood, and a supply of vinegar, wine and spirits handy for those in great pain or weak from loss of blood. A 'loblolly' brought in an empty bucket for the blood and one full of water for the sponges (it was considered more economical to have half a dozen sponges rather than clean the wounds with lint, which could only be used once). After a while the sponges would become a source of infection and the slightest wound be liable to result in an amputation. A portable stove was lit for heating tar and oils, and a kid, or half barrel, filled with hot water in which the surgeon would dip his saw and knives before operating. This was not to sterilise the instruments, but to prevent the torture of having cold metal pressed against raw flesh. Another kid was placed alongside the operating table to take the amputated limbs. Dr. Beatty and his assistants stripped to their shirts and rolled up their sleeves – they were ready to begin.

A few minutes after the crash of cannon announced the opening of the engagement, the wounded began to arrive, helped down to the cockpit by their shipmates. Most suffered their wounds with great fortitude, numb with shock, but one man was brought to the table screaming

– a large splinter of wood embedded in his stomach. The ships had not yet closed and most of the wounds had been caused by flying splinters. Close-fought actions produced less casualties than those fought at a distance. Close to, the speed of shot was so great that in penetrating the side of a ship, it produced a clean hole with few splinters. But a spent ball produced a jagged hole and splinters, which did more damage than the shot.

The man died on the table and was hastily dragged away.

The next patient was carried to the table, ashen-faced William Rivers, midshipman, his shattered left leg covered in a blood-soaked bandage. Cutting away this bandage, the surgeon briefly glanced at the wound – amputation – there was no time for a lengthy diagnosis. The badly frightened boy gulped down the proffered rum – there was no anaesthetic – closed his eyes and bit on the leather gag. One of the 'loblollies' stood behind William, arms tightly clasped round his body; another held the boy's wounded leg rigid; the assistant surgeon firmly gripped the ankle of the leg to be amputated – he had already drawn up the skin tight and applied adhesive tape circularly round the leg, two fingers below the knee. This would act as a guide for the surgeon's knife. A tourniquet was applied above the knee.

Dr. Beatty took up his position between William's legs, and in

a low voice promised him, 'in the softest terms, to treat him tenderly and finish with the utmost expedition'. True to his word, he rapidly cut to the bone with a catlin, using a circular movement, following the line of the adhesive tape. The boy broke into a sweat, and at the first touch of the saw, mercifully fainted. The surgeon sawed through both bones as quickly as possible; sewed up the stump, applied a poultice dressing and held it in place with an adhesive strap (some surgeons favoured dipping the stump in hot tar). Yet such was the remarkable skill of Dr. William Beatty, young William lived to claim his prize money.

Hours later the wounded were still coming down, the cockpit deck was full, and in places groaning and swearing men were laid one upon the other. Some prayed. One man had had a leg carried away at the pelvis by a 12 pound shot; he was carefully laid down and given a whole pannikin of rum – he would be dead within the hour. Others had been wounded by musket balls (a musket ball in the chest or stomach was considered fatal and no attempt was made to treat such a wound). Still others had been crushed by falling masts, and a dozen or more had been downed as grape shot swept the upper deck. The cockpit was a bloody shambles, the operators, smeared with blood from head to foot, looked more like butchers than surgeons – and still the wounded came!

English flagship. A great shout rang through *Redoutable*, 'A l'abordage. A l'abordage' – the French were coming. Yelling and shouting they rushed up from below, waving cutlasses and pistols, brandishing boarding pikes, only to pull up short at their ship's bulwarks. The deep recurve of the two ships' hulls caused a gap of several feet; to reach the towering topsides of *Victory* was impossible.

Yelling, 'Repel boarders', Royal Marine Captain Adair clambered into the ship's rigging followed by a party of seamen and marines. They opened up a brisk fire on the hesitating Frenchmen – panic-stricken they swarmed down the hatches to the comparative safety of the gun-decks. But the merciless fire from the French tops took its toll. Within three minutes Captain Adair and eighteen men lay dead, twenty others were wounded, many mortally. Fully-elevated 28 pounders on *Redoutable*'s main gun-deck began firing upwards, the round shot bursting through the planking of *Victory*'s upper-deck. Lieutenant Ram was mortally wounded as a shot came out of the deck at his feet, five seamen were badly lacerated by flying splinters. John Pollard, signal midshipman, suddenly seized a musket and in a blind rage began firing at the French tops. Supplied with ball-cartridges by signal-quartermaster King, he picked off the snipers every-time they rose breast high in the tops.

Redoutable was now a beaten ship, but the heroic little French captain ('Le petit Lucas' was only 4 feet 10 inches in height) refused to surrender. One young Frenchman, Midshipman Yon, climbing up the anchor chain with four ratings, actually boarded *Victory*, but they were soon cut down by overwhelming odds. *Victory* was now joined by 'Fighting' *Temeraire*, who fired a devastating broadside into the stricken French ship. Lucas said afterwards, when reporting personally to the Emperor Napoleon – 'It is impossible to describe the carnage produced by the murderous broadside of this ship. More than two hundred of our brave men were killed or wounded by it.' Broadsides from *Victory* and *Temeraire* had either smashed or dismounted all *Redoutable*'s guns, the hull was riddled, shot through from side to side, the poop

stove in, her rudder and stern-post shattered. Her decks were strewn with dead, lying amongst the debris of fallen spars, canvas, splintered masts and dismounted cannon. 300 of his 'people' killed and 222 wounded, out of a complement of 600, Captain Lucas had no choice but to strike his flag, his crew still cheering, 'Vive L'Empereur'. *Victory* cut herself clear and sheared off. It was 1400 hours. The battle continued until 16.30 hours, but Nelson had died by then, but not before he had learned of his victory. Pickled in brandy, his body was carried back to England for burial in St. Paul's Cathedral.

'Splice the mainbrace' – eagerly the crew turned to their 'tot', a gill of grog (watered rum), after the last shot had been fired. It was all over, men wandered the decks looking and enquiring for their messmates. Wreckage was cleared and damage made good, and those who had died under the surgeon's knife were brought on deck and thrown overboard. Partly demasted, her hull scarred by cannon shot, her sails in shreds, HMS *Victory* was taken in tow, her destination, Gibraltar. She had lost 57 killed and 102 had been wounded. That evening Midshipman Richard Roberts opened his 'Remark Book'. Sitting on his sea-chest in the midshipman's 'gun-room', he wrote by the light of a flickering battle lantern – 'The day of 21 October, 1805, dawned bright. . .'.

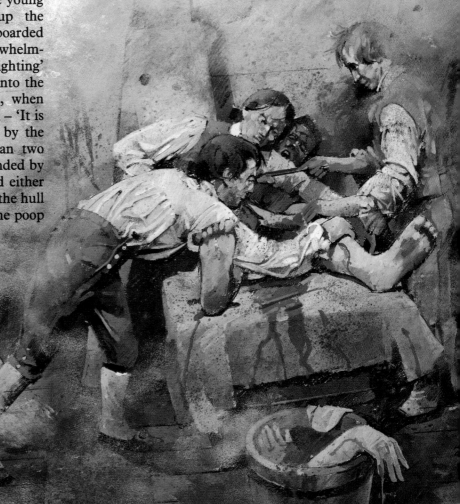

Navigation

From early times the merchant explorers of the Ancient World realised the need for navigation. It was important at all times that the captain should know the true position of his ship, which most likely had been carried off course by wind, currents and the force of the waves. To ensure that they steered a true course, a ship's navigator had to make allowance for the elements over which he knew he had no control.

Over the centuries, mariners have devised four basic methods to ensure that they arrived safely at their destinations:

Piloting

Early voyages were made hugging the coast, always keeping within sight of land. The captain would determine his position simply by watching out for landmarks; a headland, the mouth of a river, a church or temple. At night he would be on the look-out for beacons and in later times, lighthouses. Although, in the beginning, Mediterranean seafarers beached their galleys at night, sailing only by day. A coastal navigator would gradually over the years build up a mental chart – 'that temple, perched on the headland, meant that he would be in port by nightfall'. This sort of information was passed on to his successor; sometimes it was recorded in the form of charts or manuscripts, although the Phoenicians, the greatest navigators of their time, were very secretive about their methods. We still do not know how they made their landfalls with such accuracy, finding their way to Britain and eastwards beyond the Red Sea.

Should a fog come down they were totally lost, with the chance of being either swept out to sea, or driving landwards to be wrecked on shoal or rock. Other methods were needed to combat this possibility.

The title page of *The Mariner's Mirror*, 1586, by Waghenaer.

Dead Reckoning

As charts began to appear, setting down positions and distances, a navigator was able to lay a course and by working out from his speed how far he had travelled, he could establish his position. This was fine in the Mediterranean where there are steady winds, a small tidal range and gentle currents. Also, once clear of land, the Mediterranean is deep and shoal-free, with little danger of running on to submerged rocks and sand bars. The gentle currents made it possible for the navigator to estimate the distance travelled, quite accurately.

It was a different story in the often rough waters of the northern seas, with their large tidal rise and fall, vicious currents and unpredictable winds. The sailors of Britain, the Continent and Scandinavia had to feel their way across shallow, narrow waters, by hand lead and line. A lead weight attached to a long line marked off in fathoms with different coloured cloth enabled them to sound the depth of the water. The base of the lead was hollowed out and filled with tallow for examining the sea bed. An experienced mariner was able to feel his way in safety using the information supplied by his line – whether the sea bed was rock, sand or mud. The colour and smell of the ooze also helped him plot his position. This information was tabled for general use, the equivalent of the present day Admiralty Pilot books. One fifteenth-century manuscript reads: '. . . without Cille west south west of hym the ground is Rede sande and whit shellis . . . Opyn (abeam) of Dudman (Deadman's Point) in XI fadome there is rede sande and whit shellis and small blak stony . . .'

The earliest evidence of the use of lead and line dates back to the fourth century BC, Herodotus noted: 'When you get 11 fathoms and ooze on the lead, you are a day's journey from Alexandria.' Early navigation was very much a matter of common sense and observation – the direction of currents, the flight of birds, the direction of winds. Vikings sometimes took caged ravens with them on their voyages. When released, if the birds circled above the ship, the seamen knew there was no land about; but if the ravens flew off the Vikings followed them, confident that land lay close by.

At first the star's altitude was measured by extending the arm with outspread fingers, the little finger on the horizon and the thumb on the sun or star. Later, primitive instruments were devised to aid the

navigator. The cross-staff (**above**) or crossbow as the Portuguese called it; the quadrant and plumb line with a scale marked from 0° to 90° and the astrolabe. Later still the sextant was introduced. An accurate ship's chronometer was produced during the mid-eighteenth century by John Harrison, a Yorkshire carpenter. This enabled the navigator to

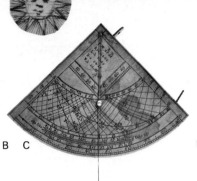

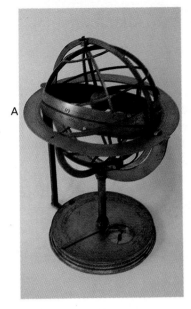

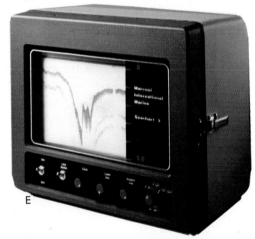

A Italian medieval Armillary sphere, 1425, representing the equator and the tropics (with a compass in the base).
B An early attempt to show the Quadrant, which was used, C, for taking angular measurements.
D The Astrolabe was used for measuring the altitude of stars.

able to steer by the sun, at night by the Pole Star – providing it was a clear night. Only on two occasions during the year does the sun bear due east on rising and due west on setting – the Spring Equinox in March and the Autumn Equinox in September. For the rest of the year allowance had to be made for a south-easterly or north-easterly rising and a south-westerly or north-westerly setting. Once a

course was established, mariners – particularly the Vikings – then used the direction of the wind and waves as indicators. They were able to obtain a fair estimate of their position, north or south, by measuring the height of the star's altitude. By measuring the height of the Pole Star it was possible to turn the daily difference in altitude into leagues and so keep a reckoning of progress.

determine the ship's longtitude by assessing the number of hours she had sailed east or west of the Greenwich Meridian in England. Using such a chronometer and the newly perfected sextant, another Yorkshireman, Captain James Cook, the most famous navigator of all time, explored

and charted vast areas of the Pacific Ocean.

Celestial Navigation
At an early stage, navigators began to check their position by determining the position of the sun and stars. This was fine in warm, sunny climes, but in the foggy, overcast northern seas this was often impossible and mariners were forced to rely more on their lead and line.

The early navigators were aware that the sun, rising in the east, followed a southerly course, finally setting in the west. They noticed that although the other stars appeared to sail across the sky, one star, the Pole Star, always remained in the north. By day they were

Electronic Navigation
To-day the navigator's task is simplified by the use of modern electronic aids. The echo-sounder (**E** above), by automatically bouncing sound waves off the ocean bed and timing their return, allows him to read depths from a screen. At night, or in a fog, radar records the bearings of ships or other objects. Inertial navigation depends for its accuracy on gyroscopes spinning at a rate of many thousand times a minute, allowing one captain of a nuclear submarine to circumnavigate the world under water. The navigator is also assisted by radio directional beams sent out from land-based transmitters. Shipboard computers, receiving information from orbiting navigational satellites, give an immediate position with great accuracy.

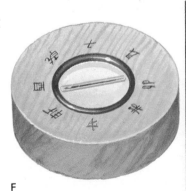

The most important single contribution to navigation, however, was the compass. Invented by the Chinese in the eleventh-century, it first appeared in Europe a hundred years later, introduced by the Arabs. This allowed mariners

to steer a true course, even in overcast weather, when it was impossible to take a reading from the sun or Pole Star. **F** At first it was simply a magnetized needle floating on a straw, in a water-filled bowl; but soon–
G it developed into a dry pi-

voted needle set into a binnacle. Accurate compass charts were being compiled, drawn on a network of rhumb lines or compass directions. Nowadays compasses are mounted in gimbals or are gyroscopic – accurate direction finders.

Acting Assistant Paymaster, William Keeler, aboard USS *Monitor*, 1862

FORTY-YEAR-old William Keeler felt distinctly queezy; perhaps Anna was right, he was too old for this sort of thing. Here he was, an officer in the Volunteer Navy of the Union – albeit only a paymaster – aboard an experimental Ironclad Battery, *Monitor*, on her way to give battle to the Southern Ironclad, CSS *Merrimack* (Virginia) in Chesapeake Bay. Yesterday they had left New York Navy Yard in fine weather, towed by the steam tug USS *Seth Low*, the sea gently lapping over their iron deck scarcely a foot above the water. *Monitor*, a strange craft that hardly resembled a ship at all, was manned solely by volunteers, all very much aware that their experimental vessel would be up against a tried and tested Confederate Ironclad more than twice her size. A wiseacre back at the Yard had christened her the 'Iron Coffin' – the name had stuck.

The ship gave a lurch to port, William, grabbing for the handrail, stumbled over Dr. Dan Logue sprawled out on the turret roof with the rest of the seasick – the ship's surgeon was past caring. It crossed William's mind that perhaps it hadn't been such a good idea to have Congressman Owen Lovejoy get him a commission in the Federal Navy – but he believed strongly in the Northern Cause and wanted to do his bit.

By noon a gale had blown up from the north-west. The wildly rolling *Monitor* was hit by a starboard sea; rushing across the deck it smashed into a port sea racing the other way – a column of spray hurtled high above the turret. A dense green roller, foaming over the bows, broke against the six feet high smoke stacks, cascading sea water down into the engine room. Thankfully the monotonous clank, clank, clank of the engines continued. But the damage had been done. Water streaming through the blower pipes had stretched the fan belts; fresh air was no longer being sucked into the engine rooms.

It was about 16.00 hours.

Eyes streaming, coughing and retching, 4th Assistant Engineer, Mark Sunstrom, lurched up the steps to the turret roof; 'Brandy', he gasped.

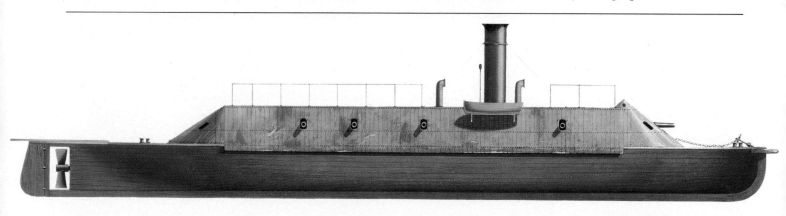

CSS *Merrimack*

The Confederates believed that the answer to the vastly superior Union fleet of steam-driven wooden warships, lay in ironclad vessels capable of withstanding the heaviest enemy shot. To save vital time, it was decided to raise the wooden warship, CSS *Merrimack*, which had been sunk in action and clad her in armour.

Proposals

To build a gun platform, close to the water thus offering the smallest possible target.
The ship to have a shallow draft – the deck to sit slightly above the water line.
To construct a casement of iron midway between bow and stern; rounded front and back, its sides sloping at 45° to the outside edge of the deck, to deflect solid shot.
The casement to have a port fore and aft, to house two specially designed 7 inch Pivoting guns. (A Confederate Lieutenant Brooke devised a way to rifle the barrels of Dahlgrens, giving them greater range and accuracy.)
The broadside to consist of 8 guns.
All action machinery and vital parts to be below the water line, safe from enemy guns.
Merrimack to be re-christened CSS *Virginia*. (During her active life as an Ironclad she was still usually referred to as the *Merrimack*.)

Action

Merrimack was cut off flush at the berth deck – 3 feet above the water line (unloaded). 2 feet thick timber was clad in 4 inch iron plate, 8 inches wide and of varying lengths, bolted on.

Specifications
Length: 263 feet
Beam: 51 feet
Draft: 19 to 21 feet
Tonnage: 3,200 tons
Speed: (Rated) 9 knots (Actual) 4 to 5 knots
Ram: 1500 pounds cast iron 2 feet long
Crew: 14 officers, 260 men.
Fuel consumption: 30 hundredweight anthracite per head
Boilers: 5 – 1294 horse power
Propeller: 2 Blade, 17 feet 4 inches diameter
Guns: fore and aft, 2 Brooke rifle 7 inch broadside, 2 Brooke rifle 6.4 inches, 6 Dahlgrens 9 inches.

The Swede's face stood out deathly pale beneath the streaks of coal dust and oil. On his way to the spirit locker William passed sailors carrying senseless firemen and engineers up top to the fresh air. Smoke, steam and gas billowing from the open bulkhead door to the engine room were already filling between decks with a stifling fog.

'There's an engineer still in there, Paymaster.'

Holding a handkerchief to his nose, William dashed into the engine room, bounding over heaps of coal and ashes, skidding on the oil-slicked deck. Robinson Hands, 3rd Assistant Engineer, lay by the port engine overcome by carbon dioxide fumes. Half suffocating, William and the Bosun's Mate, John Stocking, who had followed him in, dragged the engineer across the iron deck to the berthing space, slamming the bulkhead door shut behind them.

Once the ventilation was restarted, the engine room crew soon recovered and *Monitor* sailed on. But not before the captain, Lieutenant John Worden, had set the colours 'Union down' (upside down, a sign of distress) to call for assistance from *Monitor*'s gun boat escort. Bobbing around like corks, the gun boats could offer no help, so the Ironclad had to look out for herself.

By the following night, as they slipped into Hampton Roads to anchor, the gale had blown itself out. After a supper of soup, good beef steak and green peas, fruit, nuts and brandy, several of the officers lit up cigars and climbed to the turret roof. An occasional gun lit up the darkness, its shell bursting like a giant firework. William sat in his stateroom writing to his wife, Anna, by the light of a candle; '– vessels were leaving like a covey of frightened quails & their lights

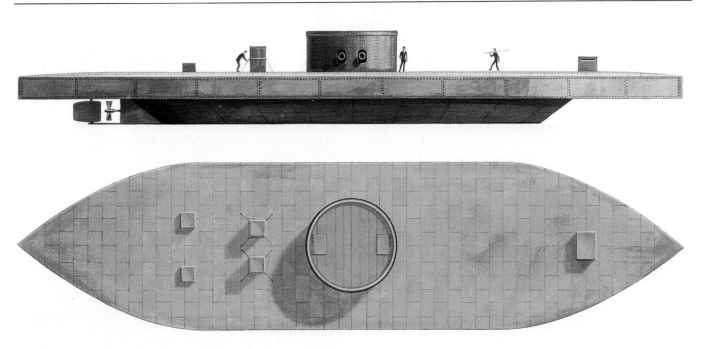

Plan and elevation of USS *Monitor*

To counteract *Merrimack*, the Union designed a purpose built Ironclad Battery, christened USS *Monitor*. Like the Confederate ship she was designed to fight low in the water, again offering the smallest possible target.

Above decks
The hull was built in two parts:
Upper section
Length: 172 feet, iron-plated, tapering to a point fore and aft.
Width: 41 feet
Lower section
hull of vessel
Length: 122 feet Wood
Width: 34 feet

The gap between the iron and the wooden hull made the penetration of shot even more difficult.

The pilot house was situated forward, just behind the anchor well. From here the Captain directed the action and the helmsman steered the ship. It was constructed of 1 foot thick iron blocks or 'Logs', 9 inches high and bolted at the corners. One block down was an inch wide aperture for observation.

Squarely amidships lay the 'Cupola' or gun-turret, a flat-topped cylindrical structure with 8 inch thick iron cladding. Two gun ports in the front of the turret allowed two 11 inch

Dahlgrens to be run out, fired, then withdrawn. The turret revolved (a major step forward in naval gunnery) giving an all round field of fire (except directly forward – the pilot house was in the way).

The turret was turned by its own steam-engine housed below decks. The *Monitor* was slightly faster than the *Merrimack* and far more manoeuvrable.

Below Decks
Below decks behind the pilot house lay the officers' wardroom (11 officers), the officers' staterooms and the Captain's cabin. Amidships was the

mens' berthing space and mess deck (48 Petty officers and men) and two stores lockers. A bulkhead door led to the engine room and coal bunkers – stowage space for 80 tons of anthracite.

Vulnerability
It was the opinion of Captain Worden that *Monitor* was vulnerable to attack by a determined boarding party, who could drive iron wedges under the turret to prevent it turning. Then, pouring water down the smoke stacks to drown the engines and stop the blower system, leave the crew the choice of surrender or suffocation.

danced over the water in all directions'.

After a fitful night dozing – all hands were kept to quarters, no one slept properly – William jerked awake to the shrill of the Bosun's pipe. The shout, 'All hands up hammocks' seemed to him a bit unnecessary. From across the bay he could clearly hear the fife and drum aboard the Confederate *Merrimack*, drumming the ship's company to quarters. He looked at his watch, 05.00, he closed his eyes again. Next thing he was being shaken by his servant; 'Half past seven, Sir, breakfast 'most ready Sir. That *Merrimack*'s coming.' Breakfast over in record time, William hurried down the turret ladder to the deck – the deck hatches had been battened down ready for action. The 'roads' were covered by an early mist, but already a warm sun was breaking through, it was going to be an unusually beautiful day. He could just make out *Merrimack* and her consorts slowly making their way from Sewall's Point. *Monitor* lay-to, a pygmy, alongside the mighty *Minnesota* who had been badly mauled and driven aground by *Merrimack* the day before. His offer of help curtly refused by *Minnesota*'s captain, Worden steamed out from the shadow of the big ship and made towards the enemy.

On deck with Dan Logue and the Captain, William watched *Merrimack* wallowing towards them, she could only be making 4 or 5 knots. If anything she appeared to be an even more grotesque sight than their own ship, but bigger, so much bigger. A puff of white smoke mushroomed from her bow port; William ducked involuntarily as a shell howled above their heads to land with a fearful crash into the side of *Minnesota*.

'Gentlemen, that is the *Merrimack*, you had better go below.' William and the surgeon needing no second warning, scampered up the ladder and were through the turret hatch in a trice.

Aboard *Merrimack* the crew were astonished at the weird vessel sailing towards them. One officer later described it as, 'Such a craft as the eyes of a seaman never looked upon before – an immense shingle (wooden roof tile) floating in the water, with a gigantic cheese box rising from its center.' Commander Catheby ap Roger Jones decided to ignore the Union Ironclad and, laying-to a mile off, began to pour shells into the helpless *Minnesota*, who returned the fire with broadsides of her own. Caught between these two ships, *Monitor* was in imminent danger of being hit by either side (during the engagement *Monitor* was in fact hit several times by shots from *Minnesota*) as they were both firing 'Line-of-sight'. Ricochet or 'Line-of-sight' firing was general practice during this period, particularly when there was an urgent need for accuracy. Shells and solid shot were 'skimmed' along the surface of the water in a series of bounces. *Monitor*'s 11 inch guns had always to be fired in this manner, since their

mounting only allowed a five degree angle of elevation. With a clang that rang throughout the ship, Captain Worden slammed shut the iron turret hatch – they were now completely cut off. A thrill of fear ran through William, was it indeed an iron coffin? Would the armour withstand *Merrimack*'s shells. Sunlight filtering through the overhead grating combined with the dim light of the battle lanterns to throw grotesque shadows of guns and gunners on to the circular turret wall. Passing down through the turret to take up his position in the pilot house forward, Worden turned to the gunners struggling to load a 175lb shot into the starboard 11 inch Dahlgren; 'Send them that with our compliments, my lads.' A profound silence reigned in the turret, they all had the same fear, would the Confederate shells smash through their iron plates? The thunder of broadsides and the howl of shells as they flew over from both sides, made the silence in the turret seem even more terrible.

Lieutenant Sam Greene, the Executive Officer in charge of the turret who sighted and fired the two Dahlgrens, turned to William; 'Paymaster, ask the Captain if I shall fire?' The speaking tube had broken down and William was acting as runner between the Captain and the turret. He scuttled forward to the pilot house to deliver the message. The bearded Worden – his beard came all the way down to his chest – was peering through the observation slit. Quartermaster, Peter Williams, was at the wheel, beside him stood Howard the Pilot.

When *Monitor* nearly foundered during the gale, sea water streamed through the blower pipes, soaking the driving belt of the fans. This stretched, lost purchase and slipped on the driving wheels, leaving the fans useless. (It also drenched the machinery that turned the turret, which in turn rusted.) Deprived of their draft, the furnaces rapidly filled the engine room with carbon dioxide and steam created from the water pouring down the smoke stacks on to the boiler fires. Once the watertight doors were opened by the escaping engine room crew, the steam, smoke and gas rolled into the rest of the ship. This was the very situation that Captain Worden feared could be brought about by a determined enemy boarding party.

As the deck of *Monitor* stood barely a foot above the surface, all her compartments were under water (William Keeler could see the waves rolling across the glass skylight set into the deckhead of his cabin, in all but the calmest of seas). A ventilation system had to be installed that pumped fresh air round the ship at a rate of 7,000 cubic feet a minute.

The air was drawn through two blower pipes on the upper deck, by fans driven by steam engines and circulated throughout the ship. As well as ventilating the living accommodation, the air was drawn into the ash pit of the boilers and up through the fires, supplying a strong draft that kept up the combustion.

33

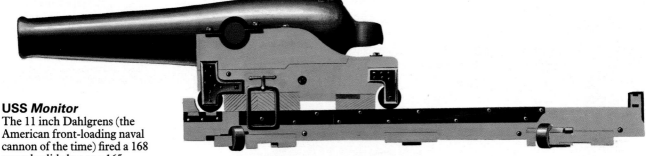

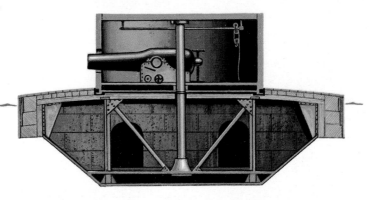

USS *Monitor*

The 11 inch Dahlgrens (the American front-loading naval cannon of the time) fired a 168 pound solid shot or a 165 pound explosive shell. The two guns fired separately, each gun port being closed as soon as its gun recoiled. No one in the turret was able to see the effect of the shots, so William was sent forward to the pilot house after each salvo to ask the Captain.

Stodder and Stimers cranked round the turret until the ports faced away from the enemy. (As a result of the soaking it received during the gale, the machinery for revolving the turret had rusted.)

Cranked back, they were sighted by Greene through the open ports. It took *Monitor*'s gunners seven to eight minutes to load, aim and fire the Dahlgrens. During the battle, lasting from 08.00 to 13.00, *Monitor* fired 41 rounds and obtained twenty hits.

As it took the whole crew to open and close the heavy iron port stoppers, a slow and laborious business, Greene decided half way through the engagement to leave them open and chance a direct hit as the turret was swinging round.

When the gun ports were closed, the gun muzzles were too close to them to allow the long-poled rammers to be used. With this in mind the designer had allowed for a small hole in the gun port stoppers, just large enough to take the handle of the rammers. At regular intervals the Confederates could see two poles running in and out of the Union gun ports.

CSS *Merrimack*

The Confederate gunners could fire each of their ten guns every five minutes, but having only shell (except for 20 rounds of undersized shot intended to be heated to act as red-hot fire balls – useless against an Ironclad) their gunnery – on the admittance of their own gunnery officers – was entirely ineffectual.

Monitor was hit 23 times, but at least two of these hits came from USS *Minnesota*.

'Tell Mr. Greene not to fire till I give the word, to be cool and deliberate, to take sure aim and not waste a shot.' A minute later the word was given and the 11 inch Dahlgrens thundered out, one at a time – the *Monitor* shuddered. Feverishly, Acting Master Louis Stodder cranked the turret round to reload.

More than once Sam Greene thought of his old friend and room-mate in the Naval Academy at Annapolis, Lieutenant Walter 'Butsy' Butt. 'Butsy' was now commanding one of the guns that were hurling shells at *Monitor*. Below the firemen were shovelling anthracite into the furnaces, squeezing every ounce of energy out of the Ironclad's engines, totally cut off from the battle raging above. Greene's crew, covered with black powder and smoke, had stripped themselves to the waist, the sweat was rolling off them. Then *Merrimack* turned her attention to *Monitor*, this irritating gnat that was peppering her with 11 inch shot – it was 08.45. Firing began at long range, but this rapidly closed to fifty yards, the two ships slowly circling each other in spirals – now opening the distance to 100 yards, then closing until they were almost touching. The fearful impact of the first hit threw the turret into confusion, the gunners stared in consternation at a big dent in the turret wall.

'Will you look there at that big dent, Sir!'

The Chief Engineer, Alban Stimers, quelled the panic, he had worked on *Monitor* during her construction.

'Big dent? Of course it made a big dent – that's just what we expected, but what do you care about that so long as it keeps out the shot?' His quiet confidence calmed down the gun's crew, soon they were boasting of whipping *Merrimack* in double quick time.

After nearly two hours of blazing away at each other very little damage had been incurred by either ship. Throughout the battle, William had scuttled between the turret and the pilot house, carrying the Captain's orders to Sam Greene. Both he and the Captain's Clerk, Toffey, who was helping him were exhausted running to and fro with a constant flow of messages.

'Tell Mr. Greene that I am going to bring him on our starboard beam close alongside (the *Merrimack*).'

'That was a good shot, went through her water line.'

'Don't let the men expose themselves, they are firing at us with rifles.'

'That last shot brought the iron from her sides.'

'She's too far off now, reserve your fire till you're sure.'

Merrimack's pilot ran her aground in shoal water, leaving the Southern ship at the mercy of *Monitor*, who ranged alongside pumping in broadside after broadside – but from a position that did not allow the enemy to reply. It was a quarter of an hour before the Confederate backed off into deep water, her propeller churning mud and sand. Time enough for Sam Greene to get in 5 or 6 salvoes at point blank range – cracking the enemy's iron plates, but not penetrating them. Captain Worden took advantage of a lull in the fighting to order William to break out the spirits – an eighth of a pint of whisky for each man.

'Look out now, they're going to run us down, give them both guns.' William raced back to pass on the Captain's message to Greene. The *Merrimack* was coming straight for them, but Commander Jones had forgotten that she had left her two foot ram in USS *Cumberland*'s wooden side the day before. So, although she caught *Monitor* a glancing blow, which set the Union ship reeling, she did no damage.

Stimers, Stodder and the other Quartermaster, Peter Truscott, were leaning against the turret wall chattering, when a shell landed directly by them. Stimers was thrown to the deck, but jumped up immediately; Stodder was flung clean over both guns and was unconscious for an hour. Poor Truscott, whose head had been only inches from the point where the shell landed, 'dropped over like a dead man' – but when he eventually regained consciousness, he was found to have suffered no permanent injury.

In the pilot house, William stood by Captain Worden as he peered out for any signs of damage to *Merrimack* – there was a sudden crash, a flash of light and the house filled with smoke. A shell had exploded directly on the observation slit. Worden staggered, covering his face with his hands, blood trickling through his fingers and down his long beard.

'My eyes, I am blind.' (Worden's face was permanently blackened by the gun powder and he lost the sight of one eye.)

The calmest man there, the Captain gave his orders. 'Gentlemen I leave it with you, do what you think best. I cannot see, but do not mind me. Save *Minnesota* if you can.'

They decided to fight on, Sam Greene took command; but the *Merrimack* had had enough, she hauled off, sending one last shell screaming over the top of *Monitor*.

Although battered and dented, neither ship had sustained any lasting damage. Ironclads were there to stay – impregnable – until the advent of the armour-piercing shell.

The only serious casualty during the action was Captain Worden, blinded in the one eye by a shell bursting on the observation slit.

The Battleship

La Gloire
1859, France

As a result of their crippling losses during the Napoleonic wars, the French Navy sought a new devastating weapon that would give them an edge over the numerically superior British Fleet. Henri Paixhans, a French artillery officer, introduced the shell-gun into naval warfare. A hollow, cast-iron sphere filled with gunpowder, smashing its way through the hull, would set a wooden ship on fire. The British countered with shell-guns of their own, mounted now in steam-powered ships driven by screw propellers. By 1855, both countries were armouring their

ships with four inch thick wrought iron plates, to produce floating batteries. The turn of the decade saw the appearance of *la Gloire*, the first true battleship, Britain replied with *Warrior*. *La Gloire* was timber-built with iron plating.

Displacement: 5617 tons
Length: 252 feet
Weight of armour: 820 tons
Thickness: 4.7 inches – waterline 4.3 inches – gun-deck
Armament: 26 × 50 pounders
Breech-loading rifled
Speed: 12 knots

HMS *Dreadnought*
1906, Great Britain

Dreadnought, by reason of her greater size and mounting more big guns, made all previous battleships obsolete. With her superior speed and long-range destructive power (her heavy guns could fire forward, aft and on the beam). In 1915, she sliced through *U29*, in the North Sea, after the U-boat had sunk four British cruisers.

Displacement: 22,000 tons
Length: 520 feet
Beam: 82 feet
Draught: 31 feet
Speed: 21 knots
Crew: 750
Armament: 10 × 12 inch; 24 × 12 pounders; 5 × torpedo tubes
Armour: 11 inch belt (the most heavily armoured part of the ship, the belt ran along her sides above and below the water line).

HMS *Thunderer*
1872, Great Britain

The main armament was now mounted in hydraulically-operated swivelling turrets, instead of broadside. Once again breaking away from age-old tradition, *Thunderer* was given an iron hull, and completely discarding sail and rigging, she relied exclusively on steam propulsion, carrying enough coal to give her a range of nearly 5,000 miles.

Displacement: 9,390 tons
Length: 285 feet
Beam: 62 feet 3 inches
Draught: 27 feet 6 inches
Speed: 14 knots
Crew: 420
Armament: 4 × 12 inch in two turrets (later 4 × 10 inch); shell 700 pounds; 6 × 6 pounders and smaller guns. Two torpedo tubes.
Armour: 14 inch plates

HMS *Hood*
1920, Great Britain

Laid down in 1916, the battle-cruiser *Hood*, 'The Mighty Hood', was unequalled for size. Lessons learned from the loss of three battle-cruisers at the Battle of Jutland, resulted in *Hood* being more heavily armoured. However, this did not prevent her being penetrated by a salvo from *Bismarck* in 1941, when her after ammunition magazine blew up, sending her to the bottom with only three survivors.

Displacement: 46,200 tons (loaded)
Length: 860 feet
Beam: 105 feet
Speed: 31 knots
Crew: 1,400
Armament: 8 × 15 inch; 12 × 5.5 inch; 4 × 4 AA; 6 torpedo tubes
Armour: 12 inch belt; 3 inch deck; 15 inch turrets

HMS *Hood*

Admiral Graf Spee
1936, Germany

Hampered by the Washington Treaty of 1919 (German battleships were restricted to a displacement of 10,000 tons – unloaded), the Kriegsmarine put three 'Pocket Battleships' on the stocks – 'Panzerschiffe'. The first, *Lützow* (formerly *Deutschland*) appeared in 1933, to be followed by *Admiral Scheer*, 1934 and *Admiral Graf Spee* in 1936. Neither battleship nor cruiser, they proved to be a great disappointment, being under-armed and armoured for the one and too slow for the other. The *Admiral Graf Spee* scuttled herself in December, 1939.

Displacement: 16,200 tons (loaded)
Length: 804 feet
Speed: 28.5 knots
Armament: 6 × 11 inch; 8 × 6 inch; 6 × 4 inch; 8 × 37 millimetre; 8 × 20 millimetre
Armour: 2.5 inch to 3.5 inch side; main turrets 5.5 inch

Admiral Graf Spee

Yamato
1941, Japan

Completely ignoring all existing naval treaties, Japan set out to build the biggest and most powerful battleships ever seen.

This resulted in the *Yamato* being launched in 1941 and her sister ship, *Musashi*, in 1942. Despite her heavy armour, she was sunk by United States' aircraft in 1945, with a loss of 3,000 lives.

Displacement: 72,800 tons (loaded)
Length: 865 feet
Speed: 27.5 knots
Armament: 9 × 18.1 inch; 12 × 6 inch; 24 × 5 inch anti-aircraft guns; 147 × 25 millimetre AA
Armour: 16.1 inch belt; 18 to 24.8 inch turrets; 7.75 inch deck

New Jersey
1943, USA

The last of the Iowa class, *New Jersey* was launched in 1943; this class was the fastest battleship ever built. Although falling short of the *Yamato* and *Musashi*, the class was the greatest of all Allied battleships. *New Jersey* first went into action with the Pacific Fleet in January, 1944, mostly in task force operations.

Displacement: 57,600 tons (loaded)
Length: 887 feet 3 inches
Beam: 108 feet
Draught: 38 feet
Speed: 33 knots

Crew: 2,700
Armament: 9 × 16 inch; 20 × 5 inch; 80 × 40 millimetre AA; 48 × 20 millimetre AA; 4 aircraft
Armour: 12.5 inch belt; 17.5 inch turrets; 4.75 inch main-deck

HMS *Vanguard*
1946, Great Britain

Vanguard was Britain's largest battleship ever and the last capital ship to be built by any navy in the world. She was just too late to take part in World War II and was scrapped in 1960 as obsolete.

Displacement: 51,420 tons (loaded)
Length: 814 feet

Beam: 108 feet
Draught: 36 feet
Speed: 29.5 knots
Crew: 1,600
Armament: 8 × 15 inch; 16 × 5.25 inch; 60 × 40 millimetre AA
Armour: 13 to 14 inch side; 13 inch main turrets

'Lofty' Williams, Stoker First Class, aboard HMS *Glasgow*, 1914

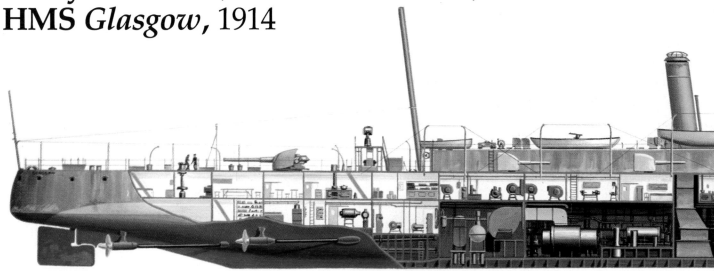

HMS *Glasgow*, 05.30 hours, 8 December, 1914.

Lofty Williams, Stoker First Class, waking to the blare of the ship's bugle, groped on top of his ventilator shaft for the stub of yesterday's final fag and lit it. With the first puff came the long-drawn shrill of the bosun's whistle – 'All hands, heave out, heave out, heave out, lash up and stow. Show a leg, show a leg, show a leg.' Reluctantly he lowered himself from his hammock and, shivering, dragged on his working rig, 'Fearnought' flannel shirt and trousers; he slipped on his stokehold clogs, wooden-soled to protect his feet against the hot plates of the boiler room deck. The ship lay at her mooring in the inner harbour at Port Stanley in the storm-ridden Falkland Islands. She was one of the two remaining ships of Rear-Admiral Sir Christopher Craddock's ill-fated squadron that had been attacked off Coronel in Chile.

The mess cook hurried to the galley with his mess tin to draw the morning cocoa, rich in sugar and condensed milk, ladled from a bubbling tub – ¾ pint each man. Skimming off the cockroaches, Lofty gulped down the steaming brew, partly to warm himself, partly from experience – invariably a scum of fat floated to the surface as 'Pusser's Kye' cooled off. He bolted down his breakfast of newly-baked bread and tinned plum jam, to leave himself time for a breath of fresh air on the upper deck before going on watch below. A 25-year-old raw-boned farmer's boy used to an open air life, Lofty fought a secret fear of working below decks under battened-down hatches.

For once it was a clear day, blue skies, even a watery sun, but bitterly cold with a piercing wind. Beyond the harbour the heaving sea, grey and angry, rolled south to the Antarctic. Within minutes Lofty, chilled to the bone, hurried below to the engine room, thankful for its sticky warmth; later, streaming with sweat, he would curse the heat. Lifting a hinged steel grating he climbed down a ladder to the stokehold, a lofty space covered by an armoured deck and dominated by two fifteen feet wide cylindrical boilers. A narrow alleyway between these boilers led to the adjacent boiler room, now cut off by a tightly battened watertight door. A handful of small electric lamps gave out a meagre light, leaving the corners of the compartment in deep shadow. Secondary lighting was supplied by a bulkhead oil lamp, kept burning at all times.

This gloomy place had a stench of its own, the smell of burnt out furnaces and grease, competing with the choking smell of coal dust. Water pipes on the fire-blistered exterior of the boilers were of highly polished copper and brass. Overhead was festooned a mass of lagged steam pipes – if these split, scalding steam would jet out, creating havoc in the confined space. The whole was covered in a thick layer of coal dust; the *Glasgow* had just finished coaling ship.

Lofty fired the port boiler, his messmate, 'Knocker' White, the starboard one. Their trimmer, Joe Hemsley, kept them supplied with coal from the two bunkers, dragging it along the plates in an iron skid – by the end of the watch he would be as black as the Ace of Spades.

The fireman going off watch grinned at Lofty. 'Enjoy your slicing and raking, mate.' Muttering to himself Lofty opened the furnace door and pushed the brightly-burning fire aside with a 'slice', a seven foot long rod of steel, flattened at the business end which weighed about one hundredweight. Next, after damping down the fire with the salt water hose, he began prising off the clinker which had formed in huge flakes on the fire bars, cutting off the flow of air to the boiler fire. It was back-breaking work and he soon stood in a pool of sweat. Hardly had he finished than the engine room telegraph clanged – 'Raise steam with all despatch.'

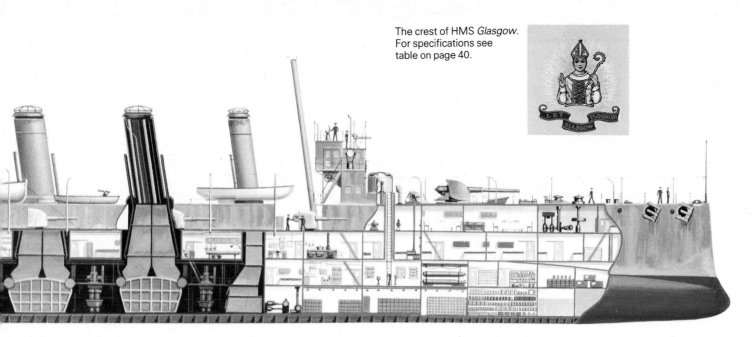

The crest of HMS *Glasgow*. For specifications see table on page 40.

It was 08.00 hours.

Stoker Chief Petty Officer Silvester lifted the hinged grating and shouted down, 'Jerry's outside. Old von Spee's been sighted heading straight for Stanley.' Feverishly Lofty shovelled in coal from the pile beside him – Joe Hemsley had been busy. Once they had got up steam and were under way, he would watch the 'Kilroy' (automatic dial) from the engine, each time it pointed to his boiler he would throw in three shovel-fuls.

When World War I broke out, Vice-Admiral Maximilian Graf von Spee, commanding the German East Asiatic Cruiser Squadron, was at Pagan Island in the Pacific Ocean. He had left the German port of Tsingtau in China, after receiving a wireless message from Berlin – 'Imminent danger of war with Great Britain, France and Russia.' Surrounded by enemies, the British, French and Australian fleets had heavy units, in both the Indian and Pacific Oceans, he now learned from a further signal that the Japanese with their powerful Navy were likely to come out on the side of the Allies.

All his ships were coal-fired, without an adequate supply of coal they became useless, and the coaling bases at his disposal would soon be overrun by the Allies. The cruisers would then have to be replenished with coal and other supplies from German merchant

A shipbuilder's scale model of the heavy cruiser *Scharnhorst*, made by Blohm and Voss to sell the design to the Kriegsmarine. The guns and fittings are modelled in German silver.

Ships at Coronel and the Falklands

German ships at both Coronel and the Falklands

Ship	Type	Year of completion	Displacement in tons	Guns: maximum range in yards	Speed in knots	Principal Armour	Complement
Gneisenau, Scharnhorst*	Armoured Cruisers	1907–8	11,400	8: 8.2″ (13,500), 6: 5.9″ (11,200)	23	6″ belt; 6″ barbettes; 7″ turrets	765
Dresden	Light Cruiser	1908	3,600	10: 4.1″ (10,500)	24	Protective plating	320
Leipzig	Light Cruiser	1906	3,200	10: 4.1″ (10,500)	22.5	Protective plating	285
Nürnberg	Light Cruiser	1908	3,400	10: 4.1″ (10,500)	23.5	Protective plating	295

British ships at Coronel

Ship	Type	Year of completion	Displacement in tons	Guns: maximum range in yards	Speed in knots	Principal Armour	Complement
Good Hope*	Armoured Cruiser	1902	14,100	2: 9.2″ (12,500), 16: 6″ (11,200)	23	6″ belt; 6″ barbettes; 5″ turrets	900
Monmouth	Armoured Cruiser	1903	9,800	14: 6″ (11,200)	22.5	4″ belt; 5″ barbettes; 6″ turrets	675
Glasgow	Light Cruiser	1911	4,800	2: 6″ (11,200), 10: 4″ (9,800)	25	Protective plating	375
Otranto	Armed Liner		12,000	8: 4.7″		Nil – did not take part in battle	

British Ships at Falklands

Ship	Type	Year of completion	Displacement in tons	Guns: maximum range in yards	Speed in knots	Principal Armour	Complement
Invincible*, Inflexible	Battle-cruisers	1908	17,250	8: 12″ (16,400), 16: 4″	25	6″ belt; 7″ barbettes; 7″ turrets	780
Carnarvon	Armoured Cruiser	1904	10,850	4: 7.5″ (12,000), 6: 6″ (11,200)	22	6″ belt; 6″ barbettes; 5″ turrets	650
Cornwall, Kent	Armoured Cruisers	1903	9,800	14: 6″ (11,200)	22.5	4″ belt; 5″ barbettes; 5″ turrets	675
Glasgow, Bristol	Light Cruisers	1911	4,800	2: 6″ (11,200), 10: 4″ (9,800)	25	Protective plating	375

Flagships

ships, in lonely anchorages – a daunting prospect. The situation looked desperate, but not hopeless – he must decide where to use his squadron to the best effect and quickly. The squadron commander looked down at the list of ships lying on his cabin desk; *Scharnhorst*, his flagship, an armoured cruiser of 11,400 tons, completed in 1908 – top speed 23 knots; and *Gneisenau*, her sister ship. Also completed in 1908 were the light cruisers *Dresden* and *Emden*, each of 3,600 tons with a top speed of 24 knots and the *Nurnberg*, 3,400 tons. A modern, powerfully efficient squadron, they were noted for the quality of their gunnery – von Spee's ship, the *Scharnhorst*, had won the Kaiser's gunnery prize two years running.

He glanced at his orders from the Kriegsmarine:

'. . . The aim of cruiser warfare is to damage enemy trade; this must be effected by engaging equal or inferior enemy forces, if necessary. . . . The conduct of the naval war in home waters must be assisted by holding as many of the enemy's ships as possible in foreign waters.'

Then he studied the instructions issued by Kaiser Wilhelm II, the Supreme War Lord:

'The peacetime sailing orders for ships (abroad) became invalid from the moment that an officer in command has an assurance that a war has broken out in which the German Empire is taking part. From that moment he must make his decisions in the sense of these orders. . . . Above all things, the officer must bear in mind that his chief duty is to damage the enemy as severely as possible. . . . Much more will depend on an officer, when he is in command of a ship operating independently in foreign waters, than is usually the case. The constant strain will exhaust the energy of the crew; the heavy responsibility of the officer in command will be increased by the isolated position of his ship; rumours of all kinds and the advice of apparently well-meaning persons will sometimes make the position appear hopeless. But he must never show one moment of weakness; he must constantly bear in mind that the efficiency of the crew and their capacity to endure privations and dangers depend chiefly on his personality, his energy and in the manner in which he does his duty.'

After a conference with his captains, Admiral von Spee decided to steam east across the Pacific to carry cruiser warfare to the west coast of America. Not only did the British have an extensive mercantile trade plying along that coast, but there was every chance of obtaining a regular supply of coal in Chilean ports. In the words of the Kriegsmarine, 'Chile is a friendly neutral.' The light cruiser *Emden* was sent into the Indian Ocean to create havoc among the British shipping there – which she did, sinking or capturing 23 vessels in 70 days. Finally she was beached and forced to surrender on 9 November, 1914.

By 18 October the German squadron was sailing from Easter Island, where they had coaled from supply ships for the last leg of their journey to the west coast of America. They also replenished their supply of fresh meat, buying it from a British rancher who had no idea that war had been declared. Warned of the approach of the German warships, Rear-Admiral Craddock had sailed his antiquated heavy cruisers, *Good Hope* and *Monmouth*, manned mainly by scratch crews, to meet them. He also had the *Otranto*, an armed merchant cruiser with him and the light cruiser, *Glasgow*, the only modern warship under his command. (As von Spee sent out all his radio transmissions from the *Leipzig*, the British admiral believed that he was steaming to do battle with a single German light cruiser.) The *Glasgow*, scouting ahead, warned Craddock by radio that there was more than one ship, but he nevertheless decided to attack, although his position was hopeless – he had plenty of time in which to turn south and escape.

They met off Coronel on 1 November: at 19.00 hours, von Spee ordered his ships to open fire. It was soon over. The German cruisers were too much for the British ships. The old *Good Hope* went down at 19.57 hours, with all hands, including Kit Craddock – *Monmouth* at 20.54 hours.

Staring into the roaring furnace, stoking like mad to get up steam, Lofty Williams's mind went back to that dreadful day off Coronel. Battened down below, he remembered with horror each shudder as *Glasgow* let off a salvo; the crash as she took a four inch shell below the water line; the panic rising in him at the thought of being trapped in the stokehold if she should capsize and sink. But *Glasgow*, together with *Otranto*, had got away to fight another day. This time it would be different. The 12 inch guns of the battlecruisers *Invincible* and *Inflexible*, supported by armoured cruisers *Carnarvon*, *Cornwall* and *Kent*, must surely be too much for the German squadron. *Glasgow*, with a

'Forlorn Hope', the unfortunate title of the *Good Hope*'s magazine, proved to be only too appropriate.

Forlorn Hope

Victualling a ship

At the beginning of the First World War, the Royal Navy was still employing a system of victualling dating back to the time of Nelson's 'Wooden walls'. The Paymaster's department, responsible for administering the *Glasgow*, only issued enough food for one midday meal per man, per day – and then only in its raw state. Each man was allowed a quantity of meat, half a pound of newly-baked bread or 'hard tack' (ship's biscuit) potatoes and dried peas. In addition cocoa, tea, sugar and hot water were supplied, sufficient for a man's needs. This was supplemented by a daily allowance of a few pence, which, at a pinch, enabled the lower-deck hand to eat more than once a day.

The galley, overseen by the ship's cook and his mates, contained a coal-fired cooking range and the necessary 'mess traps' – pots, pans and so on – to boil, bake or steam anything within reason. It was the job of the duty mess cooks to prepare the food for cooking. In a mess of a dozen or so men, two chosen in rota each day (one from the port watch, one from the starboard watch) to draw rations and prepare the food for the galley. A Leading Hand acted as mess caterer; he controlled the messing allowance and by the use of regulation chits (settled at the end of each month) he could draw from the Paymaster's store or canteen, bacon, beans, jam or whatever else took his messmates' fancy.

He would draw the daily issue of fresh meat from the ship's butcher, being careful to have it weighed in front of him. Rarely a joint, the meat was usually a cheap cut of fat, lean with a fair amount of bone. It was a common practice for the mess cooks to chop this into small pieces, place it in a tin dish, cover it with dough and have it either baked or boiled – pie or pudding! Supper was the responsibility of the individual and there was fierce competition, even sometimes brawling, for the use of the frying pans and the cooking range – woe betide anyone frying a kipper if the others wanted rashers of bacon. The cook's mate in charge of the galley in the evening had not only to be a diplomat, but big and tough.

However, the seamen of the lower-deck were a hardy lot and few went hungry.

grudge to settle and her sister ship, *Bristol*, would also do good work – provided the Fleet was not trapped in harbour by von Spee – still coaling! The Commander of the Fleet, Vice-Admiral Sir Doveton Sturdee, an officer with a reputation for coolness, gave orders to raise steam with all despatch – then went down to a good breakfast. Sturdee's fleet had sailed from Devonport on 11 November, arriving at Port Stanley on 7 December.

Following his victory at Coronel, Vice-Admiral von Spee was advised by the Kriegsmarine to round Cape Horn into the Atlantic and make for home. Their main concern was to get the cruiser squadron safely back to Germany. On 27 November the squadron ran into a violent storm. Gale force winds whipped the sea into a fury, sending mountainous waves crashing over the bows of the cruisers: shifting the coal piled on the decks. The shoots and scuttles became blocked, so that the water foaming across the decks could not escape. At times with three feet of water trapped on the upper deck, the ships were in danger of capsizing. There was nothing else for it, the precious coal had to be shovelled overboard – the seamen hanging grimly on to life lines, as each successive wave surged over them. Battered, but still in fighting trim, they rounded the dreaded Horn on 1 December and set a course north into the Atlantic.

On 6 December, after having received an inaccurate intelligence report that there were no British warships in the Falklands area, he decided to attack Port Stanley to destroy the wireless station and set fire to the coal dumps, so necessary to the British South Atlantic Fleet. Bitter opposition came from three of his captains, Maerker of *Gneisenau*, Ludecke of *Dresden* and Haun of *Leipzig*. They pressed von Spee to pass the Falklands well to the east – the damage that could be inflicted did not justify putting the squadron at risk – but the Admiral was adamant. The raid was to be carried out by *Gneisenau* and *Nurnburg*, the other ships would give support. The worst fears of von Spee's captains were realised at 09.00 hours on the 8th when his ships were less than ten miles from Port Stanley. A shout came from Korvettenkapitan Busch, high in the control position on the foremast of the *Gneisenau*. He reported four triangular masts in the harbour – this could mean only one thing, British battle-cruisers.

Coaling ship

Coaling ship was a dirty job, a chore resented and detested, by officers and men alike, for everyone was involved. Everyone that is except the stokers, who strangely enough were allowed to lounge about smoking whilst the rest of the ship's company turned to. It was felt that they would see enough of the coal once they were down in the stokehold.

The *Glasgow* coaled in the biting chill of a sub-Antarctic night, lit up as if for a Fleet Review. The collier had been tied alongside for some time and the merchant seamen could be heard shouting and cursing as they set up the derricks and made ready the winches. Aboard the *Glasgow*, the bunker lids were removed from circular apertures about two feet across, both on the upper deck and in a corresponding position on the lower deck and a chute rigged up to take the coal through to the bunkers.

In theory these chutes, made of heavy steel, consisted of two halves that could be easily clamped together to form a hollow cylinder. But over the years, persuasion with a fourteen pound hammer had knocked them out of shape, making the operation long and

frustrating. Once the coal began dropping through, the dust would squirt from the gaps and cracks, covering everywhere with a thick, black film. Paper was pasted over the air vents in a vain attempt to prevent the coal dust finding its way on to the mess decks – it failed miserably.

Coal sacks, capable of holding two cwt, were filled in the hold of the collier, hoisted aboard the cruiser on derricks and dumped on the deck. There they were immediately seized by the working parties, shoved on to wheel porter's barrows, wheeled to the chutes and tipped down into the bunkers. Every filled bag was counted and every so often one was weighed. This monotonous and back-breaking work went on throughout the night and soon an all-pervading fog of coal dust penetrated every nook and cranny of the ship, setting the crew choking and coughing. It was dawn before the bunkers were filled and the dog-tired, black-faced ship's company left to wash and clean up the ship. They were just relaxing over breakfast, a distasteful chore behind them, when the alarm gun went off, the signal was run up – 'Enemy in sight.'

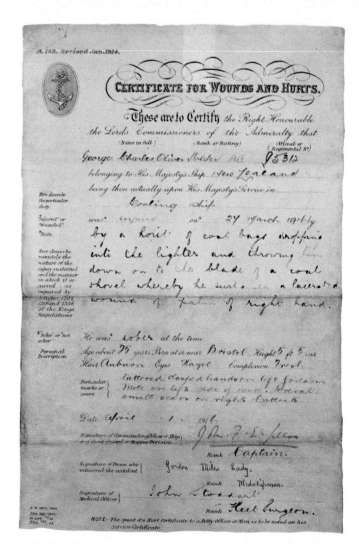

A First World War wound certificate.

Signal lamps flashed from *Scharnhorst*; von Spee ordered a change of course to the south-east, hoping to find an enveloping mist. Had he known the British Fleet was still coaling, he might well have attacked the ships at their moorings. It was 09.30 hours. At 09.45 hours *Glasgow* was the first to leave harbour. On the bridge, Captain Luce, still bitter about Coronel and determined to fight his ship to the last shell, watched the smoke trails of the Germans making for the horizon. By 10.00 hours Sturdee was in hot pursuit, his battle-cruisers five knots faster than von Spee's ships. In almost perfect weather the British fleet would be able to bring its guns to bear within two hours. Flags ran up *Invincible*'s signal halyards, the signal – 'Chase'. With his infinitely superior armament, Sturdee knew that he had von Spee's squadron at his mercy – at 11.32 hours he signalled that ships' companies would have time for a meal before action commenced. Officers and men would fight better on a full stomach. At 12.47 hours the signal 'Open fire and engage the enemy' was made. The 12 inch guns roared out, straddling the German cruisers. Realising that his squadron was doomed, von Spee signalled his light

cruisers *Dresden*, *Leipzig* and *Nurnburg* to 'Leave line and try to escape.' Then, showing the same courage as Craddock at Coronel, he turned his armoured cruisers *Scharnhorst* and *Gneisenau* east-north-east and attacked the British.

In his stokehold Lofty braced himself as the *Glasgow* heeled over in a tight turn to starboard; they were after the light cruisers. It was punishing work keeping up 26 knots, his arms and back ached, the fierce heat from the roaring fire beat back at him every time he opened the furnace door. An excessive roll of the ship threw the door back on him, badly scorching his arm; but, wiping the sweat away from his face with a handful of cotton waste, he carried on.

At 14.50 hours he felt *Glasgow* shudder, they were in action, the six inch guns were at work. Shutting out his fears, Lofty blindly shovelled in coal. A sudden blinding flash and roar, coal flew everywhere, steam jetted from a split pipe – a four inch shell had hit the starboard bunker. Lofty glanced anxiously at his mate: 'Knocker', shaken but unhurt, stared in disbelief at his shattered boiler, his face stained yellow by the fumes of the lyddite shell. Joe Hemsley, luckily in

the port bunker at the time, was buried in an avalanche of coal – several tons – but he crawled out in one piece, even managed a sickly grin. The starboard boiler was closed down, but they continued to stoke the port one.

At 20.30 hours the hinged grating was raised, a grinning stoker Chief Petty Officer Silvester poked his head through, 'It's all over, *Leipzig*'s sinking, Kent has gone after *Nurnberg* and *Dresden*'s escaped in a rain squall. Go up top for a breather.' Ignoring the mist and slanting rain, the stokehold crew sucked in the fresh air as soon as they reached the upper deck. Close by, silhouetted in *Glasgow*'s searchlight, the remaining crew of *Leipzig* lined the rails singing the 'Song of the Sea', waiting for the British lifeboats to rescue them. But before the boats could reach the stricken ship, she heeled over to port and rapidly sank by the bows – only seven officers and eleven ratings were picked up.

Although desperately sorry for the German sailors, the stoker could not help feeling a sense of pride at the victory; but most of all Lofty Williams felt thankful to be alive.

Herbert Hermann, Mechanikersobergefreiter, *U47*.

'Taffy' Davies, Corporal Marine, HMS *Royal Oak*, 1939

So NOW they knew. Not even the wildest of the buzzes that had been flying round the German submarine, *U47*, since she had left Kiel on 8 October, 1939, had come anywhere near the truth. The crew had sensed that they were going on a special mission, but why only twelve torpedoes instead of the usual fourteen? Why were they only partially fuelled – why only a fortnight's supplies? Why had the number of bottles of lemonade been cut so drastically? A U-boat tour of operation usually lasted four to five weeks – later, the schnorkel boats would be able to stay out for up to nine months. 'Sea Cows', giant supply U-boats, brought out supplies to them.

Ten minutes ago, at 04.45 hours, all hands had been piped to the forward torpedo space – the 'House of Lords' – all 39 of them; crammed against the bulkheads, crouching on the bunks. The expectant buzz died out as Kapitanleutnant Gunther Prien, the U-boat commander ducked through the bulkhead door, carrying aerial photographs and a chart. He looked intently at each man in turn – the tension was unbearable.

'To-night we're going into Scapa Flow.'

He had intended to break the news gently, in a prepared speech, but face to face with his crew, he decided on the spur of the moment to come straight out with it. After the first gasp of amazement, it went deadly quiet as the crew took in the commander's words. Wan-faced under the harsh electric lamps they stared at each other in horror. Get into the impregnable British naval base in the Orkneys – and then get out?

'Now listen, I'll get you in there and we'll sink aircraft carriers, battleships, cruisers – ' Prien tried hard to appear confident, but he only made it worse;

you could touch the fear. He went on: 'The Oberkommando der Kriegsmarine doesn't give us much hope of getting back, but I promise you,' he stared round again, 'I promise you I will get you out.' The crew were not convinced, this had to be a one way ticket. Twice it had been tried in the First World War and both U-boats had been sunk. The best they could hope for was to be taken prisoner to rot out the war in a P.O.W. camp.

The first thought that flew into Mechanikersobergefreiter Herbert Hermann's mind was – 'If only I'd gone to *U45*'. This was his first trip and it looked like being his last. Prien had eagerly snapped him up to join *U47* – Herbert had finished top of his class of 52 at the Submarine Training School. But a comrade, Willi Tank, who had passed out ahead of him had objected. Prien had remained adamant, so Herbert had joined *U47*, Willi, *U45*. (*U45* sailed a fortnight later and disappeared without trace.) He was badly scared, he did not want to die so young. His usually boistrous mess-mates, all old hands, now sat silently, gloomily sipping their beer ration. It was specially brewed beer, but it still did not keep very long – it soon 'grew strings' inside the bottle. Herbert was undecided whether or not to drink his; he was bound to bring it up when they surfaced. The young torpedoman had been miserably seasick every night since leaving Kiel. They had travelled only at night, on the surface, ploughing their way through heaving seas whipped up by a gale force wind. During the daytime they had lain on the shallow, sandy bottom of the North Sea – mercifully the boat did not roll down there.

He gulped down his beer.

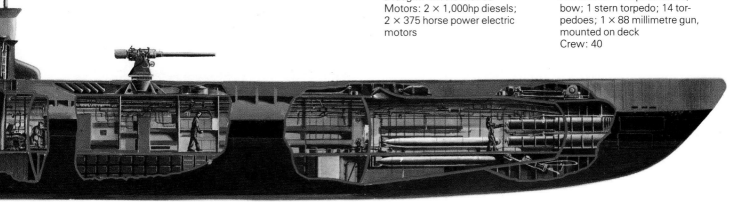

Statistics of *U47*

Launched: 29 October 1938
In service: 17 December 1938
Displacement: surface, 753 metric tons
submerged, 857 metric tons
Length: 66.5 metres
Width: 6.2/4.7 metres
Draught: 4.7/9.5 metres
Motors: 2 × 1,000hp diesels; 2 × 375 horse power electric motors

Speed: surface, 17.2 knots; submerged, 8 knots
Range: surface, 6,500 sea miles at 12 knots; submerged, 72 sea miles at 4 knots
Diving depth: 100/200 metres
Fuel: 108 metric tons
Armament: 4 torpedo tubes, bow; 1 stern torpedo; 14 torpedoes; 1 × 88 millimetre gun, mounted on deck
Crew: 40

Life aboard a U-boat

German U-boats were designed for action not comfort, that was subordinated to fighting ability. Unlike the British and Americans, who built their submarines to last 20 years, the German U-boats were only designed to last through a war – very few did, many, at the height of the anti-U-boat campaign, failed to return from their first operation.

There was very little space on a long voyage. Clothing and personal belongings were stowed wherever possible, behind pipes, under bunks, in any odd corner – every inch of space was filled. At the beginning of a long voyage, food and provisions were stacked along the cramped passageways to form a false deck, which gradually disappeared as the operation went on. After being submerged for several hours the air became foul with the stench of fuel oil, cooking, sweat and in particularly rough weather – vomit. This was only relieved when the hatches were open on the surface, clearing the air in the boat; until the next dive.

The food aboard U-boats was the best that could be provided, and on some, meals were accompanied by music played from records – although they were usually forbidden American and British popular music and jazz. Clothing was varied and optional, but everyone on surface watch in foul weather stuck to the official cold weather leather gear and oilskins.

Discipline varied from boat to boat, according to the personality of the captain. One U-boat commander punished minor offences by depriving a man of cigarettes for a number of days; or if he helped himself to more than his fair share of food – a fortnight in 'Coventry'. On the other hand, stealing a packet of cigarettes on *U606* could lead to a spell in prison, or being packed off to the Russian Front – *U606* was not a happy boat.

Statistics of HMS *Royal Oak*

Completed: 1914
Displacement: 29,150 tons
Fully loaded: 33,000 tons
Crew: 1146
Length: 620 feet
Beam: 102 feet
Draught: 28.5 feet
Speed: 23 knots
Armament: 8 × 15 inch; 12 × 6 inch; 8 × 4 inch AA guns; 4 × 3 pounders; 5 × machine guns; 10 × Lewis guns; 4 × 21 inch torpedo tubes
Armour: armoured belt – 13 inch; main turrets – 13 inch.

He was beginning to wonder why he had joined the U-boat Arm. A regular sailor, enlisting in the Deutsche Kriegsmarine in 1938, at the age of seventeen, he had only recently qualified as a torpedoman. Firstly they had put him through a stiff medical – the naval surgeons paying particular attention to ears, nose and throat – he had passed A.1. Then his training had commenced. German torpedo hands were expected to be craftsmen, spending most of their time in the schoolroom dismantling and reassembling 'Tin fish'. He vividly remembered the first time he had seen the hundreds of parts laid out on a bench – but he had soon learned.

Fiejte Walz, the boat's cook (the ship's company were lucky, Fiejte had once been a chef in one of Hamburg's finest restaurants) came round with an issue of 25 cigarettes and a large bar of chocolate. 'Skipper's compliments. Got to be stowed in your Davis apparatus.' The old hands grinned, if they 'bought it' the chocolate would not be much good tucked away in their Davis apparatus – they might just as well eat it now. But Fiejte's next remark stopped them, 'I shouldn't if I were you. The "Old Man's" coming round to check, anyone caught is on a charge.'

At 17.00 hours they had a 'Hangman's Meal' – the best on the boat, though few had any appetite. U-boats' crews had the best of everything – roasts – pork, beef, veal and chicken – smoked eel, bacon, fresh and tinned fruit and eggs – in the case of the *U47*, prepared by a master chef in a minute galley. To-night was no exception and it was served on blue-edged crockery – officers had the same food, but eaten off red and gold-edged plates. At the commencement of every voyage each member of the ship's company was issued with two soup plates, two dinner plates and two cups – they usually lasted about a fortnight, then they ate straight from tins. Commander Prien had a passion for eggs, but would never use his authority to insist on having them – he made a point of eating exactly the same as his crew. As the youngest rating aboard *U47*, nineteen-year old Herbert had to serve the offices and petty officers before he could sit down to his.

The forward torpedo space where he messed was crowded. Four torpedoes were carried in the tubes, ready for firing; four below the deck plates and two secured on top of the deck plates. A wooden top balanced on these served as a mess table. As Herbert once wrote home, 'We squat like Arabs until two torpedoes have been fired'. He furtively rubbed his smooth chin, his other messmates were already sprouting a healthy stubble – no one, from the 'Old Man' down shaved on an operation, just washed themselves the best they could in sea water with a special soap, an itchy, scum-ridden affair.

The meal over they had prepared for action. Bunks (these were never cold; as the ratings going on watch

Glims Holm

1

3

2

H.M.S. *Royal Oak* •

St. Marys

Lamb Holm

Burry Island

Holm Sound

U47's route into Scapa Flow

1 First torpedoes fired

2 Rear torpedo fired

3 Second torpedoes fired

Rose Ness

got out, those coming off watch got in) were clipped back to the bulkhead, the four torpedoes hoisted from below the deck plates and secured on their rails for rapid reloading. All traces of messing vanished, it was now the main fighting platform of the boat.

It was 18.57 hours.

The alarm clanged throughout the boat – 'Battle stations. Battle stations' blared from the voice pipes. Herbert and Willi Loh raced aft to their battle station at the stern torpedo – number five – located between the electric motors. In the control room Kapitänleutnant Prien ordered, 'Stand by to surface.' The bright lights were switched off, leaving the dim red glow of the secondary lighting. The bridge look-outs had already donned their red spectacles to accustom themselves to the darkness outside the boat. Pushing back the peak of his cap the commander took his position at the periscope – 'Periscope depth'.

Oberleutnant (Ing) Wessels, the engineer officer, took the boat up with precision. One metre – two metres – three metres – up to periscope depth. 'Up periscope' – it slid silently from its housing below the deck. Prien swung the periscope through a rapid 360 degrees, slammed up the handles and ordered – 'Surface. Down periscope'. Compressed air hissed from the pipes, the water noisily gurgled out of the ballast tanks. 'Hatch of conning tower above water', called Wessels.

British sailors celebrate on board a captured U-boat.

Prien, night glasses round his neck, already climbing the ladder, unclipped the hatch; sea water and bitterly cold air rushed in, the latter sucked into the boat by the newly-started diesel engines. (The crew gratefully gulped down the fresh, salt air – by now the air in the boat had become uncomfortably stale.) Immediately the look-outs began to call out –

'Starboard – nothing.'

'Port – nothing.'

'Aft – nothing.'

Prien peered ahead of the boat through his glasses. Satisfied, he called into the voice pipe, 'Both engines full ahead.' The bow wave lifted as they made 17 knots – they were on their way to Scapa Flow.

Leaning on the stern tube, Herbert was beginning to feel ill – the rolling of the boat, the thud of the engines, the smell of diesel oil, smoke and Fiejte's cabbage were too much for him. For the benefit of the crew below, the commander was giving a running commentary over the voice pipe.

'Strong Northern Lights in the distance are throwing the islands into sharp relief – it's like day, but the shadows being cast are a nuisance. South Ronalsay is on our port side, beyond I can see Ward Hill, the highest point in Scapa Flow.'

Desperately Herbert fought the rising gorge, concentrating on Prien's every word.

'We are close in to Mainland Island on our starboard side, running up to Kirk Sound.' The commander's voice faltered, then, 'Where are the other damn blockships? I can see only one . . .' He was cut off by Maschinershauptgefreiter, Erwin Holzer, calling from the echo-sounder – '2 metres – 1 metre – half a metre.' The crew braced themselves against the shudder of the boat as she crunched into the sand.

'Hard a starboard. Full ahead' – The commander's voice was still calm. They had strayed into the shallow Skerry Sound – it looked as if they would not get into Scapa Flow after all. For agonising seconds the racing diesels roared without effect, then slowly, *U47* began to inch forward – 1 metre – 2 metres – 3 metres. They were in clear water.

The boat's clock registered 00.15 hours.

Prien sounded relieved – 'That was close, but we are on course now, just going into Kirk Sound. St. Mary's village is almost on top of us – quiet as the grave; they must be dead not to hear us.' Prien ordered – 'Stop diesels. Half ahead group up.'

The heavy, penetrating thud of the diesels gave way to a thin high whine as the electric motors cut in. Cautiously he steered the boat towards the two northern blockships; he intended to slip between them. Anxiously he peered through the darkness, with only a few centimetres of water under his keel, even at high tide, it was going to be touch and go. The boat, caught by the fierce current in the narrow, confined

The torpedoes used by *U47* to sink *Royal Oak* were a new improved version of the Whitehead torpedo of 1868. Weighing around 1½ tons (one fifth of which was explosive charge) they were 7 metres long 53 centimetres in diameter. Battery-powered electric motors sent them streaking through the water at 40 knots, to tear holes in the battleship large enough to drive a bus through. Previously torpedo engines had been driven by compressed air, but this had the disadvantage of leaving a tell-tale trail of bubbles in its wake.

Running
A shaft transmitted power to gears in the stern of the torpedo, which turned two propellers – one rotating clockwise, the other anti-clockwise – this stopped the 'fish' spinning. A gyroscope, sensitive to the slightest change in direction, controlled rudders attached to a pair of vertical fins, keeping the torpedo on course. A pressure-sensing diaphragm on the torpedo's casing, regulating two horizontal fins, maintained the correct depth, to ensure striking the *Royal Oak* below her armoured blister.

As a trigger mechanism protruding from the snout of the torpedo smashed into the side of the battleship, it detonated the explosive charge, blasting a gaping hole. As guard against a premature explosion blowing the *U47* out of the water, a small propeller controlling a safety lock, spun itself off a threaded shaft and fell away after about 30 metres.

channel, was yawling to right and left. A loud scraping noise echoed through the length of the boat, they had fouled the anchor chain of one of the blockships, an old sailing vessel. It seemed an age as it clanged down the side of *U47* – then silence – they were through into the Flow.

'Mechanikersobergefreiter Hermann to the bridge with the aim optic' – the 'Old Man' sounded quite jovial. Grabbing the heavy machine for aiming the torpedoes, Herbert struggled with it up the swaying conning tower ladder to the open bridge. He gasped – the sky was alight with changing colours, like fingers, like searchlights probing upwards. Scapa Flow appeared to be empty – where were the warships? Once again at his battle station, he continued to listen to Prien's clipped words as they scoured the Flow for a target – he suddenly realised that he did not feel seasick.

'Single-funnel battleship ahead, 3,000 metres' – Prien's voice was excited. Hastily thumbing through the recognition silhouettes, he continued, 'It's of the Royal Sovereign class, probably *Royal Oak*.'

'Prepare for surface firing.'

'Tubes one to four ready' – called Ober-mechanikersmaat Bleek.

'Depth seven metres – Fire one' – the boat lurched, the first torpedo was running.

'Tube two at the ready' – 1.2 seconds later the order came – 'Fire two.' 3.5 seconds later, 'Fire three.' The three deadly tin fish, fanning out, raced towards the sleeping battleship. The fourth tube had jammed.

Three minutes passed – nothing. Misfires? (The torpedoes they had taken aboard were the new, electrically-powered ones, rather than the usual torpedoes powered by compressed air; these left a tell-tale trail of air bubbles in their wake.) Or had they missed completely? The commander swung the boat round to fire the stern torpedo. Gripping the hand control, Herbert waited the order to fire. 'Fire five' – he jammed down – the boat lurched, the stern torpedo was on its way.

Loh and Herbert raced to the forward torpedo space, their heavy sea boots ringing on the metal deck plates.

Prien was already steering *U47* towards Kirk Sound, when the First Officer, Oberleutnant zur See, Englebert Endrass – 'Little, but no nerves at all' – persuaded him to turn back and have another go. Three forward torpedoes were loaded in record time, manhandled, there was no time for cranking in. Within seconds they were cutting through the water, set to explode below the battleship's armoured blister. The order was given, 'Hard a starboard. Full ahead'. At 17 knots they were again making for Kirk Sound and home.

There were one – two – three flashes; three hits. As Prien announced it a great shout rang through the boat.

'Shut up' – Prien was violently angry, Herbert had never heard him shout before.

'Do you want everyone in Scapa Flow to hear us?' It was 01.22 hours.

Aboard the *Royal Oak*, Norman, 'Taffy' Davies, Royal Marine Corporal, captain of X turret 15 inch gun, lay in his hammock writing a letter. He put it down and looked at his watch, it was just after 01.00 hours, time to turn in. He had hardly rolled over when a dull boom had him sitting up, a violent tremor ran through the ship. A couple of minutes later, Marine Corporal 'Dingle' Combes, Corporal of the Gangway, passed on his way to get his cocoa, 'Pusser's Kye'. He had heard a rumour that the CO_2 machine had exploded. Not at all happy, Taffy crawled out of his hammock and dressed. (Peacetime routine was maintained on battleships even after war had begun, no one was allowed on the upper deck unless properly dressed – tunic, polished boots and cap.) He went up top to have a look for himself. It was pitch black, the aurora borialis had finished for the time being. He took out a packet of Craven A cigarettes, lit up and strolled forward on the port side, he could hear the clink of hammers on the forecastle – something was definitely up. A passing stoker stopped him: 'What the hell's going on, Royal?'

Taffy told him about the CO_2 machine, but the

Ship's Log

8/10/39 11.00 Heligoland Bight. Wind SE.1. Cloudy.
Left port (Kiel) on special operations. . . .

9/10/39 South of Dogger Bank. Wind SSE 4–5. Overcast, very dark night.
Lying submerged. After dark, surfaced and proceeded on our way.
Met rather a lot of fishing vessels.

10/10/39 North of Dogger Bank. Wind ESE 7. Overcast.
During day lay submerged; at night continued on course.

11/10/39 Devil's Hole. Wind ESE 7–8, Overcast.
As on previous day.

12/10/39 Wind SE 7–6, Overcast.
During day lay submerged off Orkneys. Surfaced in the evening and came into coast in order to fix exact position of ship. From 22.00 to 22.30 the English are kind enough to switch on all the coastal lights so that I can obtain the most exact fix.

13/10/39 E of Orkney Islands. Wind NNE 3–4, light clouds, very clear night, Northern Lights on entire horizon.
At 04.37 lying submerged in 90 metres of water. Rest period for crew.
At 16.00 general stand to. After breakfast at 17.00, preparations for attack on Scapa Flow. . . .
Kirk Sound is clearly visible. It is a very eerie sight. On land everything is dark, high in the sky are flickering Northern Lights, so that the bay, surrounded by highish mountains, is directly lit up from above. The blockships lie in the sound, ghostly as the wings of a theatre.
. . . In the meantime I had decided to pass the blockships on the Northern side. On a course of 270 I pass a two-masted schooner . . . with 15 metres to spare. In the next minute the boat is turned by the current to starboard. At the same time I recognise the cable of the northern blockship at an angle of 45 degrees ahead. Port engine stopped, starboard engine slow ahead, and rudder hard to port, the boat slowly touches bottom. The stern still touches the cable, the boat becomes free, it is pulled round to port and brought on to course again with rapid manoeuvring, but we are in Scapa Flow.

14/10/39 00.27.
. . . We proceed north by the coast. Two battleships are lying there at anchor (Prien mistook the old seaplane-carrier, *Pegasus*, for the battleship, HMS *Repulse*, in fact *Repulse* was not in Scapa Flow at the time), and further inshore, destroyers. Cruisers not visible, therefore attack on the big battleships. Distance apart 3,000 metres. 00.58 – Estimated depth, 7.5 metres. Impact firing. One torpedo fixed on the northern ship, two on the southern (in fact four torpedoes were loaded, one failed to leave the tube).
01.21 – About! Torpedo fired from stern; in the bow three torpedoes are loaded. After three minutes comes the detonation on the nearer ship. There is a loud explosion, roar and rumbling. . . .
01.28 – At high speed both engines we withdraw.

stoker had just come from there and there had been no explosion in the engine room. (The stern torpedo from *U47* had hit the anchor chain and the noise and tremor had been caused by the cable running out of the chain locker.)

As he flipped the stub of his Craven A over the side, there was a tremendous explosion from starboard, followed by another and another; he grabbed for the guard rail, flung sideways as the ship heeled over to port. Water cascaded down, soaking him to the skin. Almost immediately the 'Old Girl' heeled over to starboard, taking on a 30 degree list – Taffy knew she was going down, settling over all the time, the list increasing. 'Make your way aft to the *Daisy*' – an officer shouted from the forecastle. (The *Daisy* was a small fishing drifter tied up on the port quarter of the *Royal Oak* – used for taking liberty men to and from shore and bringing on supplies.) Taffy staggered aft along the dangerously sloping deck – before he had reached the quarter-deck it had increased to 60 degrees. A panic-stricken Maltese petty officer steward crouched clutching a broken arm, wildly praying to his patron saint. Taffy helped him down to the quarterdeck ten feet below, the ladder had gone. The 'Malt', over the rail in a trice, jumped into the sea and swam for the drifter. Taffy cleared the guard rail, walked down the ship's side to the armoured blister and leapt for the rail of the *Daisy*. Willing hands pulled him inboard.

The *Royal Oak* had heeled over to an angle of 80 degrees; it flashed through his mind that it would only need a seagull to perch on her yards and over she'd go. Scores of men sat along the ship's port side, still unable to believe that she was going down.

'Don't cast off, *Daisy*', they were shouting.

'For heaven's sake cast off, skipper,' shouted the survivors on the *Daisy*, 'or we'll go down with her.'

A young midshipman was calling, 'Wait for the order to abandon ship.' The men muttered and cursed, 'Listen to him, the stupid young fool', but they did – they were 'Pusser Navy', regulars with service behind them, an order was an order. Skipper Gapp gave orders to cast off the drifter, put her slowly astern and stood by to pick up survivors. There came a fearful rumbling noise from within the *Royal Oak*; as the shell room came to the top the 15 inch 'projies', each weighing over a ton, rolled from their bins, smashing their way through the stricken ship. Now only her barnacled keel remained above water, one or two men still clinging to it. Then gracefully she settled down and slowly sank. Only eight minutes had elapsed since she had been hit; hundreds of men were trapped below. There had been no time to raise the huge armoured hatches, battened down against the possibility of an air raid.

For nearly two hours the *Daisy*'s crew pulled survivors aboard; men suffering from shock, exhaustion – wet and frozen, dripping fuel oil. With more than 300 men aboard the tiny fishing vessel, Skipper Gapp gave the heart-breaking order to pull away for fear of capsizing, leaving shrieking men in the icy water. For years Taffy Davies dreamed of their shrieks – 'Don't leave us, *Daisy*'.

Barely 400 survived, 833 perished. *U47* had got in and out of Scapa Flow without being detected, an achievement believed at the time to be impossible.

Evolution of the submarine

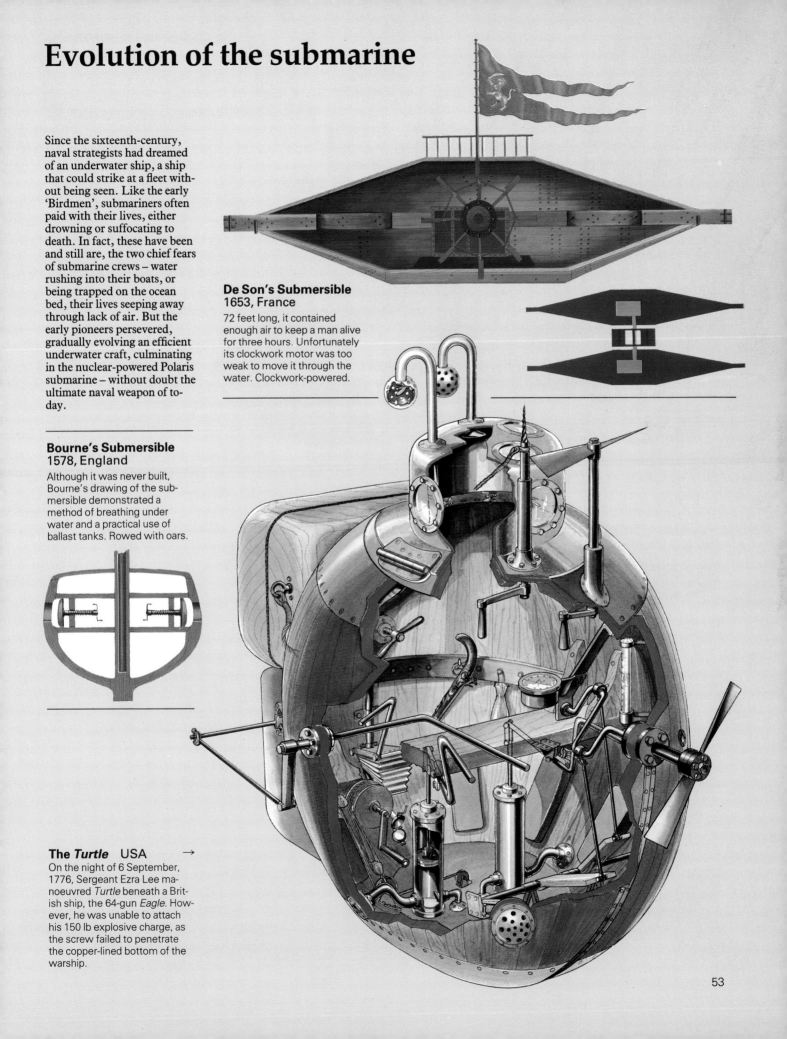

Since the sixteenth-century, naval strategists had dreamed of an underwater ship, a ship that could strike at a fleet without being seen. Like the early 'Birdmen', submariners often paid with their lives, either drowning or suffocating to death. In fact, these have been and still are, the two chief fears of submarine crews – water rushing into their boats, or being trapped on the ocean bed, their lives seeping away through lack of air. But the early pioneers persevered, gradually evolving an efficient underwater craft, culminating in the nuclear-powered Polaris submarine – without doubt the ultimate naval weapon of to-day.

Bourne's Submersible
1578, England

Although it was never built, Bourne's drawing of the submersible demonstrated a method of breathing under water and a practical use of ballast tanks. Rowed with oars.

De Son's Submersible
1653, France

72 feet long, it contained enough air to keep a man alive for three hours. Unfortunately its clockwork motor was too weak to move it through the water. Clockwork-powered.

The *Turtle* USA →

On the night of 6 September, 1776, Sergeant Ezra Lee manoeuvred *Turtle* beneath a British ship, the 64-gun *Eagle*. However, he was unable to attach his 150 lb explosive charge, as the screw failed to penetrate the copper-lined bottom of the warship.

Nautilus
1801, USA.

Robert Fulton, given a grant of 10,000 francs by Napoleon, produced a practical underwater craft with conning tower, diving planes and flooding valves. It carried a crew of three, but was never used in action. Man-powered.

Plongeur Marin
1858, Germany

Wilhelm Bauer's 'Sea Diver' was used against the Danes and although it caused no damage, it kept their fleet at a respectful distance. It had ballast tanks and was dived in a series of dips, by alternating the position of a heavy weight. Bauer and his men made the first escape from under water. Man-powered.

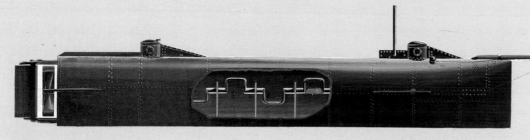

The First Attack
CSS *Hunley*

This all-metal submarine, a modified iron boiler, was almost 40 feet long and submerged by means of water ballast and weights. She was manned by a crew of eight, who hand-cranked a propeller shaft to achieve a speed of over 3 knots. She was another 'jinx boat' – 26 Confederates were drowned during trials, including Captain Hunley her designer.

On a moonless night in February, 1864, the submarine steered towards the Union warship, *Housatonic*, lying-to outside Charleston Harbour. At first the crew of the *Housatonic* mistook the Hunley for a piece of driftwood, a fatal mistake that was to cost them their ship.

There was a blinding flash as the submarine's spar torpedo went off, exploding the Union ship's magazine. The steam sloop sank, losing 5 men. *Hunley* went down with all hands.

Peral
1886, Spain

Isaac Peral introduced the electric motor into his submarine, which was a practical attack vessel firing a torpedo. Powered by 420 electric batteries.

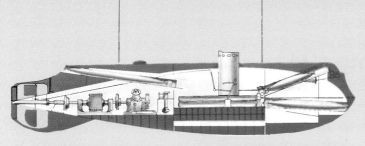

USS *Holland (SS-1)* ↑
1900, USA

John P. Holland's first successful submarine *SS-1*, led to further designs used by America during World War I.
Surfaced: Petrol engine.
Submerged: Electric motor.

U-boats (Unterseeboote) ↓
1914 onwards, Germany

By now the submarine was a powerful weapon. *U31* of 1914, had two torpedo tubes in the bow and two in the stern.
Surfaced: Diesel engines, 8 knots.
Submerged: Electric motors, 5 knots.

Sourcouf ↑
France

Between the wars nations began to build bigger submarines. The French *Sourcouf* was the biggest, displacing 4,304 tons submerged. She was 361 feet long, with a surface speed of 18 knots and an underwater speed of 8 knots. She carried two 8 inch guns; 8 × 21.7 inch torpedoes and 4 × 15.7 inch torpedoes.

The Disastrous K-Boats British →

Built to keep up with the fleet, rather than lurking at periscope depth waiting to attack from ambush, the K-Boats could reach a speed of 24 knots on the surface. The 17 built had two oil-fired steam turbine engines, each with a separate funnel, which had to be folded down just before diving. A number of tragic accidents occurred during their short active service life, mainly through collisions and mechanical failure. With a length of 338 feet, displacing 2,650 tons when submerged, they were the biggest submarines of World War I. The K-Boats were also the most heavily armed, mounting 2 deck guns and no less than 10 × 18 inch torpedo tubes.

George Washington USA

This was the first nuclear-powered submarine to be armed with Polaris ballistic missiles – she carried 16, each with a nuclear warhead. As the furthest point inland is only 1,700 miles from the sea, there is no city in the world safe from a Polaris attack.

The Polaris missile (see left of right-hand illustration), which can be fired from the sea bed, is made up of two rockets, one above the other – the nuclear warhead is carried in the nose of the top one. The rockets are ejected under immense pressure through an opening in the deck of the submarine to the surface. As soon as the Polaris reaches the air, the bottom rocket is fired electronically. After a time this falls away when the other rocket is ignited; computers guide it, together with its deadly warhead, on to its target. The other missile shown is the later Poseidon. They would never be installed together.

Sub-Lieutenant Wilson, Fleet Air Arm at Matapan, 1941

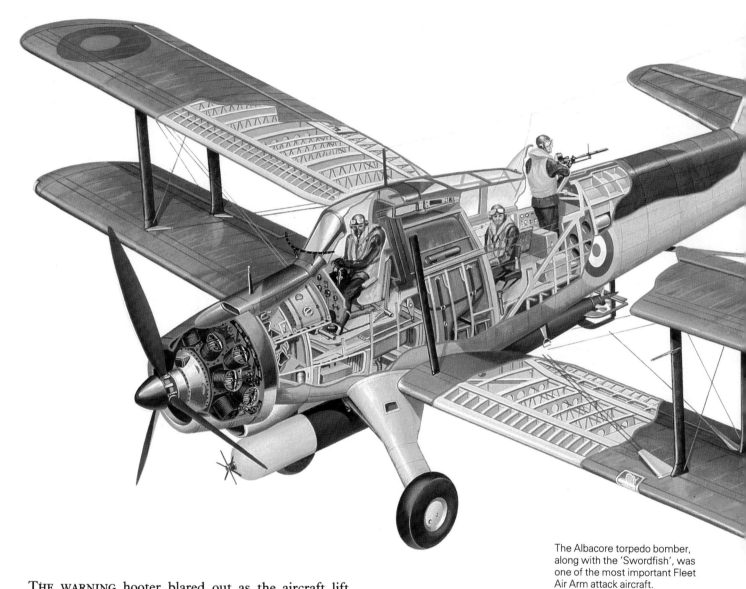

The Albacore torpedo bomber, along with the 'Swordfish', was one of the most important Fleet Air Arm attack aircraft.

THE WARNING hooter blared out as the aircraft lift rumbled up the after lift well to flight deck level. Speedily the last of the Albacore strike aircraft was pushed into position for take-off; the Commanding Officer's '4A', ranged in front, would be the first off the deck. Beneath each plane was slung a sinister-looking 18 inch torpedo, a fifth of its weight high explosive, enough to rip any warship apart. One by one the planes had been unshackled from their wire moorings in the hanger deck and pushed, wings folded, on to the aircraft lift. With 826 squadron arranged in take-off order – brakes on – the wings were now opened and locked rigid by aircraft fitters. The aircraft handling party had already jammed wedge-shaped wooden chocks under the wheels.

At 17.10 hours, the aircraft carrier HMS *Formidable*

turned into wind, and was soon making 30 knots into a 24 knot wind. The British Fleet were off Cape Matapan in the Mediterranean. Sub-Lieutenant 'Steady' Tuke, FAA pilot, in helmet and Sidcot jacket, his No. 5 uniform trousers tucked into flying boots, was carried by the wind towards his Albacore, '4P'. His parachute had been placed in position in the forward seat of the plane by a parachute packer. Clambering aboard he carried out his cockpit checks and pressed the starter button; a sharp crack and the detonated engine roared into life. The slip stream from the propeller plucked at the faded blue, well 'dhobied' overalls of Able Seaman Alf Potter, as he crouched over the chocks wedged beneath the starboard wheel

Aerial Torpedoes

First used when naval flying was in its infancy, the aerial torpedo went on to become the most effective airborne weapon against shipping. The original torpedo, designed by Whitehead in 1862, had a speed of 6 knots; by 1941, the torpedoes dropped by *Formidable*'s Albacores were cutting through the water at over 30 knots. The range had been extended from several hundred yards to over 4,000 yards, with a far more accurate and reliable directional gyro system.

Although the development of the aerial torpedo had come a long way since its first successful use at Gallipoli in 1915 (two Short 184 seaplanes, operating from their tender 'Ben-my-Chree', then hit and damaged two Turkish supply ships with 14 inch torpedoes fired from 400 yards) it was still unreliable at the beginning of World War II. Unless the torpedo was dropped from around 50 feet, the aircraft lumbering in at 90 knots, it was liable to break its back if released too high and skip along the surface if released too low. Often the delicate guiding system was damaged by the shock of impact with the water, causing the torpedo to dive to the bottom, or veer wildly off course. In many instances the exploders, added to the nose of the torpedo, failed to explode the warhead, rendering a potentially damaging hit totally ineffectual.

By the time of the Pacific battles of 1942 against the Japanese, the Americans had perfected a reliable aerial torpedo which solved these problems – the US Mk 13.

of the Albacore, one wary eye on the whirling blades. Less than a month ago one of his messmates had stepped back into a running airscrew – Alf hoped never to see anything like it again.

Sub-Lieutenant (A) 'Tug', Wilson, RNVR, the observer of '4P', sat in the 'ready room' at the foot of the port side of the island, listening to the Commander Ops' briefing. The Squadron CO had just finished explaining his proposed method of attack. They were going after an Italian fleet, 45 miles ahead and making for the naval base of Taranto at 19 knots. After the attack they were to proceed independently to Maleme on the north-west coast of Crete. Yesterday, at midday, an RAF Sunderland flying boat out of Kalafrana had sighted the Italians steaming towards Crete, on their way to destroy a British troop convoy in the area. Immediately the Navy had despatched the *Formidable* and three battleships – *Warspite*, *Barham* and *Valiant* – from Alexandria in Egypt to intercept the enemy.

At 15.10 hours in the afternoon of the 28th, 3 Albacores and 2 Swordfish of 829 squadron and 2 Fulmars of 803, made a determined torpedo attack on the Italian Fleet. The 41,000 ton battleship, *Vittorio Veneto*, had been hit and was now limping back to her home port, screened by six heavy cruisers and eleven destroyers. It was proposed that 826 squadron should attack the enemy whilst his ships were outlined against the setting sun.

At 23, the Sub-Lieutenant was already a veteran, with some torpedo runs to his credit, as well as dive bombing attacks. But this was something different, never before had a torpedo attack been attempted from a carrier at night, it was anyone's guess what would happen. He thought back to that day, the 27th January it had been, when his pilot, Sub-Lieutenant Bradshaw, had brought '4R' in too fast. The Albacore had bounced, missed the arrester wires and skidding over *Formidable*'s first crash barrier, ploughed to rest beneath the second one. The aircraft had been a complete 'write off'. Luckily they had both got away with a few gashes, but it had been close, far too close.

Commander Ops read out the last weather report,

Statistics of HMS *Formidable*

Commissioned: August, 1939.	Beam: 95 feet.
Displacement: 23,000 tons.	Draught: 24 feet.
Crew: 1,600.	Guns: 16 × 4.5 inch.
Length: 753 feet.	Speed: 30 knots.

Statistics of US *Mk 13*
Warhead: 600lb high explosive.
Length: 13 feet.
Diameter: 22.42 inches.
Speed: over 40 knots.
Weight: approx. 1 ton.
Range: several miles.

told them of the ship's intentions (course and speed whilst the aircraft were away), gave them the last known enemy position (there was no radar in the aircraft, that came later, towards the end of 1942) and wished them luck – the briefing was over.

'Tug' Wilson, as he ducked through the door to the flight deck, was met by a fierce 30 knot wind which blew him towards the parked Albacores, now revving up for take-off. Cautiously, clutching his navigator's bag containing chart-board, calculator, pencils, rubbers and compasses, he made his way to '4P'. He smiled as he remembered the story of the young, newly-joined observer to 826 going on his first anti-submarine patrol. His plane, the only one, had been ranged aft almost at the stern end of the flight deck. The carrier turned into wind, the Commander Flying gave the 'green' – nothing happened – the ship continued steaming into wind, 180 degrees wide of its

Sub-Lieutenant 'Tug' Wilson in observer's flying gear.

proper course. There was panic on the bridge, the carrier was rapidly leaving the rest of the Fleet behind. The FDO ran across the deck to ask the pilot what had happened (there was no VHF radio at that time). The observer was missing – they found him, standing by the island door, waiting for the aircraft to taxi up for him. He had thought it too windy to walk down the deck with all his gear – it had cost him a 'rocket' from the ship's captain and a fortnight's extra duties.

Avoiding the rapidly spinning propeller was always a nerve-wracking business – mercifully the deck was not greasy. Having scrambled up to his seat astern of the pilot, the Flight Deck Officer (FDO) could now signal 'chocks away'. The Commander Flying gave the 'green' from the bridge, down went the FDO's arm and the CO's Albacore was racing down the deck. Quickly '4P' was pushed into position, 'Steady' Tuke roared the engine, on the brakes, the FDO signalled and they were off, hurtling forward through the exhaust fumes of the leading aircraft. Airborne as they reached the island, he caught a glimpse of Commander Ops holding up a blackboard on which was chalked the very last-minute ship's position.

Now they were climbing to their formation position astern of the CO. His observer had set a course

directly into the setting sun, the sky was an overall bright orange. 'Tug' shouted their course to the pilot through the Gosport speaking tube; the roar of the engine made essential communication difficult, light conversation impossible. Sometimes the Gosport became unplugged, then it became necessary to pass the pilot written messages at the end of a cleft stick. It took the FDO less than five minutes to get the six Albacores of 826 squadron and the two Swordfish of 829, airborne. It was 17.35 hours.

At 2,000 feet the strike force levelled out, heading north-west towards the Italian Fleet. As it was still daylight when the enemy was sighted, Lieutenant Commander Saunt ordered the squadron to 'stooge' around in sub-flights at 500 feet, until he gave the order to attack. He was waiting for the exact moment when the sun would slip below the horizon, the moment that would silhouette their target against the western sky – whilst they themselves would be unseen. Then he would lead the squadron in, their aircraft skimming the wave tops as they attacked. A lone Walrus was circling high above the enemy fleet, her observer, Lieutenant Commander Bolt busily radioing information to Admiral Sir Andrew Cunningham, the British Commander in Chief, aboard his flagship, HMS *Warspite*.

Aboard the damaged *Vittorio Veneto*, the Italian Commander in Chief, Admiral Angelo Iachino, gazed anxiously astern through the gathering dusk. The British torpedo bombers were flying backwards and forwards beyond the range of his guns, hovering like great black birds of prey, ready to pounce at the last flicker of the dying sun. The sky turned from violet to a leaden grey as darkness slowly descended. At 19.15 hours Admiral Iachino ordered an alteration of course to 30 degrees to port – he hoped the manoeuvre, going unnoticed in the growing darkness, would allow him to slip away from the menacing torpedo bombers – his fleet was now steaming due west. The crews of the Italian ships, already at action stations manning their guns, were ready to throw up what they hoped would prove to be an impenetrable barrage. At 19.30 hours, the rearmost destroyer *Alpino* reported – 'Aircraft now coming in.' Iachino ordered – 'Make smoke'; the ships on the port and starboard wings of the Fleet switched on their searchlights, directed to dazzle the incoming pilots.

Previously, at 19.25 hours, Lt. Commander Saunt had waggled the wings of his Albacore, dived, levelled out at 50 feet and turned the nose of his aircraft towards the Italian Fleet. His sub flights followed him in. There were now ten aircraft in the attack, they had been joined by two land-based Swordfish from Maleme. From their position behind the CO, 'Tug' Wilson had a good view of what was to come – it looked a pretty daunting prospect. The searchlights revealed great blankets of smoke rolling towards the British planes. Then, at 3,000 yards, the Italians opened up with everything they had – the whole sky was lit with gunfire. *Vittorio Veneto* threw up a splash curtain with her 15 inch main armament – 4.7 inch anti-aircraft guns opened up a deafening barrage, pom-poms hosepiped a deadly hail of 37 millimetre shells. Even more frightening was the stream of red, white and green tracer that looped at them from the 20 millimetre Bredas. It crossed 'Tug' Wilson's mind, with surprise, that these were the colours of the Italian flag. The blanket barrage looked spectacular, deadly and impassable – the British planes turned away, split up and came in again singly from different directions.

Although spectacular, the barrage of fire put up by the Italians was not very effective and resulted in a number of their ships hitting each other, but did little damage to the attacking aircraft. The Albacores and Swordfish pushing home their attacks were hampered by the smoke and searchlights and no hits were registered. 'Steady' Tuke took '4P' in close, the slipstream whipping up a trail of spray as the Albacore raced over the surface of the water. He released the torpedo – nothing happened – it must have jammed. Banking sharply through the flack bursts, he circled and came in again – again the torpedo failed to drop. 'We'll have one more go,' he shouted through the Gosport. Once again he went in, the Albacore shuddering as she ran the gauntlet of exploding AA shells. Third time was not lucky; he turned away, they were close enough to see the tense, white faces of the Italian gunners – the 18 inch torpedo was still slung below the aircraft.

'That's it – it's Maleme for us.'

At 19.45 hours, Lieutenant Saunt called off the attack. But one pilot had still to go in. One minute later, at 19.46 hours, Sub-Lieutenant Williams in Albacore '5A', flying just above the surface, pressed home his attack and released his 'tin fish'. It streaked towards the 11,500 ton heavy cruiser, *Pola*, hitting her amidships on the starboard side. All electrical power gone, with three compartments flooded, her engines useless, the cruiser pulled out of line and stopped. Williams turned to follow the others to Maleme, pursued by a vengeful hail of shell and tracer. '5A', carrying a Telegraphist/Air Gunner, instead of a long range tank, ran out of fuel off the coast of Crete. The fuel gauge wildly flickering below the empty mark, the engine began to cough, they were never going to make it – Williams looked round for somewhere to 'ditch' the plane. A mile or so ahead a ship was silhouetted

against the sky, a destroyer . . . Italian, German or British? It made very little difference, they could fly no further, the pilot put the Albacore into a glide to hit the water as close to the destroyer as possible. He was relieved to hear the shout from Midshipman Davis through the Gosport, 'It's one of ours. I can see the White Ensign' – it was HMS *Juno*. The Albacore, sent up a wake of spray as she skidded along the surface to come to rest alongside *Juno*. The crew scrambled onto the wing, to await the ship's cutter, already chugging towards them – they did not even get their feet wet.

It was a relieved Admiral Iachino who watched the FAA planes break off the engagement at 19.45 hours and head due east, their exhaust flames gradually disappearing into the night. He ordered the searchlights switched off; the ships ceased to make smoke, speed was raised to 19 knots. There had been no report of damage from his fleet, so he was unaware that *Pola* was stopped, yawling in the swell, completely at the mercy of the oncoming British battlefleet.

It was not until 20.15 hours that the Italian admiral learned that *Pola* had been hit and was stopped. Believing that the British battleships had given up the

chase and were heading back to Alexandria, he had no hesitation in going to the rescue of *Pola*. At 20.18 hours, the First Cruiser Division (Heavy cruisers, *Zara* and *Fiume*, 11,500 tons and four destroyers) under Vice-Admiral Cattaneo were ordered back to assist the stricken cruiser. Straight towards the British battlefleet, closing at a combined speed of 36 knots.

The opposing ships met at 22.27 hours. Within three minutes the damage had been done – 15 inch salvoes from the three British battleships left *Zara* and *Fiume* sinking. The destroyers *Alfieri* and *Pola* were sunk by torpedoes, but not until the crew of the latter had been taken aboard British ships. The fast destroyers *Oriani*, *Gioberti* and *Cadducci* escaped to the south-west at over 33 knots, but the luckless *Cadducci* was caught and sunk. Had the Italian Cruiser Division had radar, they would have been able to detect the British ships in time to turn north-west and escape – their faster ships showing the enemy a clean pair of heels.

As they came in to land at Maleme, 'Tug' Wilson glanced at his watch – 21.45 hours, they had been in the air four hours and fifteen minutes. Throughout the flight to Crete he was unable to rid his mind of the fact they had a live torpedo slung beneath the plane. Neither he nor the pilot knew what had gone wrong. For all they knew, the thing might be armed and ready to go off the moment they touched down. He only hoped that 'Steady' would make a good landing – true

Signals given by Deck-Landing Officer (Batsman)

Once the Affirmative flag, a
white cross on a red ground,
had been hoisted, the FAA pilot
came under the direction of the
Deck-Landing Officer, the 'Batsman', who used the following
signals to bring him down
safely. The flight deck was approached directly from astern
with plenty of engine, nose well
up, the aircraft–hanging from its
propeller–slowly sinking towards the deck, arrester hook
down.

1 You are coming in on a true
   course – everything OK.
2 Your landing hook is not
   down.
3 You are coming in too slowly
   – increase speed.
4 You are coming in too fast –
   slow down.
5 You are coming in too low,
   gain height.
6 Cut engine and land.
7 Your approach is bad – go
   round again.
8 Move over this way.

to his nickname, he did. The aircraft had hardly
finished taxiing, when both men leapt out, relieved to
be safely down.

After a spartan meal and a fitful night's sleep, they
took-off next morning at 07.30 hours, landing on time
aboard *Formidable*, 09.45 hours. The CO took-off
down wind, his Albacore lightly-loaded for a two and a
half hour flight. The airstrip was short, but long
enough for a lightly-loaded Albacore, but an Albacore
loaded with a torpedo? Orders from *Formidable* had
been quite clear, bring back the torpedo – it was an
expensive item. When it came to his turn, 'Steady'
Tuke revved up and '4P' raced across the grass
towards the perimeter. At the very end of the runway
stood a sandbagged machine gun emplacement, its
gunners cheerfully waving to the departing aircraft.
'4P' hurtled closer and closer; Wilson realised they

Arrested Landing

From the very first deck
landing, made in 1911 with an
approach speed of 40mph, it
was realised that a method was
needed to slow down an
aircraft to enable it to land
safely on the restricted length
of a flight deck. When Ely
landed on USS *Pennsylvania*,
the arrester system consisted
of 22 ropes stretched across
the flight deck from port to
starboard, raised from the
deck by wooden blocks. A
50lb sandbag was tied to each
end of all 22 arrester ropes.
Fitted between the main
wheels of the Curtiss Albany
Flyer, three pairs of grapnel
hooks caught in the arrester
ropes as the aircraft skimmed
across the deck, bringing it to
a halt 50ft from the end of the
flight deck. This system, with
constant modifications and
improvements, became the
standard method of deck
landing until the advent of
vertical take-off aircraft.

Although experiments were
carried out with a number of
other arrester systems – one
being the use of longitudinal
arrester wires running fore
and aft – they were, by and
large, unsuccessful and naval
flyers reverted to the original
idea. By the time of Matapan,
arrester systems had become
more efficient. Even though
landing at much higher
speeds, the introduction of
wheel brakes on aircraft and
the development of
hydraulically controlled
arresting wires made deck
landing considerably less
hazardous.

By now every two sets of
arrester wires had their own
hydraulic arresting unit. As
the landing hook caught and
drew out an arrester wire from
its drums, a piston forced
hydraulic fluid along a
cylinder through a small hole
into a pressure tank filled

Position of arrester wires during landing

were not lifting. The waving turned to panic, the gun's crew flinging themselves sideways as '4P' brushed the top of the sandbags – the Albacore shuddered, but became airborne. Clipping the sandbags had taken off the tail wheel and part of the rudder.

09.45 hours saw the squadron circling *Formidable* awaiting permission to land. One by one they touched down without incident. '4P' was to land last of all, as there was some doubt whether the end of the torpedo would clear the deck without a tail wheel. Should it hit the flight deck it might well go off. 'Steady' Tuke took the Albacore round and made his landing approach from the stern. It seemed unnaturally hot in the cabin to Wilson, his mouth went dry, he began to sweat. As the flight deck loomed up, his only thought was for the live torpedo slung beneath them, would it clear the deck? The affirmative flag was visible at the stern of the island, another flew from the port after boom – they were cleared for landing. The batsman – always an ex-pilot – had signalled that their arrester hook was fully down. He stood at the end of the flight deck on the port side, protected by a wind-break, a safety net slung alongside the cat walk to his right – ready should an aircraft come in off course. Eight arrester wires were positioned across the length of the flight deck, ready-raised to catch the plane's hook. Beyond them stood two wire crash barriers, raised to prevent the Albacore going off the forward end of the flight deck, should she miss all the arrester wires. Asbestos-clad firemen were stationed by the island door; the 'goofers' gallery' on the bridge was packed with fellow flyers, no doubt as anxious as 'Tug' himself.

The batsman, who had been holding his bats straight out at arm's length, suddenly raised them to form a V – they were coming in too low. The pilot lifted the nose of the aircraft, but the batsman, still not satisfied, waved him round with a circular movement of his right bat. The engine, throttled down for landing, roared into life as 'Steady' revved up, the plane zoomed over the carrier, feet above the deck. They came in for their second approach, the batsman lowered his bats slightly, the aircraft was too high – they would bounce, miss the arrester wires and end up in the crash barriers. The pilot took her down slightly – the bats were straight out – yards only from the flight deck the batsman crossed his bats low down – this was it. The pilot cut the engine, the Albacore dropped like a stone, a sudden violent jerk, they had hooked on first time. The nose dropped, as the racing Albacore was pulled to a halt by the hydraulically controlled arrester wire – the tail dropped with a gentle thud. They were safely down for the second time. Thankfully the two FAA flyers clambered to the deck; already a maintenance crew was pushing '4P' towards the after lift well. By to-morrow she would be airborne again – with another mission to fly.

with air. The aircraft, racing across the deck, continuing to draw out the wire, forced more and more fluid into the tank and compressed the air. Once the hook was released after landing, the compressed air forced the hydraulic fluid back into its cylinder, returning the arrester wire to its normal position wound round the drums.

Aircraft at sea

The cannon, introduced into naval warfare during the Middle Ages, proved to be a turning point in war at sea. Fleets began to rely more and more on gunnery and a ship's fighting potential was reckoned by the number and calibre of the guns she carried. By the beginning of the twentieth-century, battleships of upwards of 30,000 tons, whose guns ranged from 12 to 18 inches in calibre, were considered the ultimate in sea power – then came the aeroplane.

From a modest beginning, aircraft began to develop at an alarming rate and by the start of World War I (1914–18), they were already being regarded as the weapons of the future. Far-seeing naval officers, quick to see their potential as a striking force, with a range far beyond that of the biggest gun, clamoured for specially designed ships to allow aircraft to operate at sea. At first, however, they were considered to be a purely defensive weapon by naval planners; Captain Sueter, Director of the Royal Navy Air Department, defined their role as:

1 Distant reconnaissance work with the fleet at sea.
2 Reconnaissance work off enemy's coasts, working from detached cruisers or special aeroplane ships.
3 Assisting destroyers to detect and destroy submarines.

4 Detecting mine layers at work or mines already laid.
5 Locating hostile craft in waters which have to be kept clear for our war and merchant vessels.
6 Assisting submarines in their look-out for vessels to attack.

7 Screening our fleets and harbours from observation by hostile aircraft by attacking the latter.
8 Preventing attacks on Dockyards, Magazines, Oil Storage Tanks, etc. by hostile aircraft.

Captain Eugene Ely in a Curtiss-Pusher makes the first deck-landing aboard the American cruiser USS *Pennsylvania* in 1911.

When a few days before the outbreak of war, Flight Lieutenant Longmore made the first torpedo 'drop' from a Short seaplane, he opened up a new role for naval aircraft. By the end of the war they had become a lethal, long-range attack weapon.

HMS *Ark Royal*

Short 184 sea-plane

Between the wars there was a race among major powers, in particular America, Britain and Japan, to build bigger and better aircraft carriers and more efficient, specialised naval planes. Yet, at the beginning of World War II, there were many naval leaders who still considered the battleship as invulnerable to attack from the air. The havoc caused by the Japanese naval flyers at Pearl Harbor and their sinking of the battleships *Repulse* and *Prince of Wales*, changed all that. Later, at the Pacific battle of Midway, neither fleet saw each other, the 14 inch guns of the capital ships were as useless as muskets. Although the battle lasted 48 hours, it was won in five minutes when American carrier-borne dive bombers swooped down on the Japanese aircraft carriers.

The aircraft carrier remained supreme until the advent of the next ultimate weapon – the guided missile. These made the gigantic post-war aircraft carriers (the US *Nimitz* displaced 82,000 tons) hopelessly vulnerable targets; this, together with spiralling costs deterred the building of such ships. However, there still remained a need for air power at sea, but the introduction of Vertical Take-Off Aircraft and the use of helicopters, has removed the need for vast flight decks.

Early Advances

In November, 1910, an American, Eugene Ely, took-off in a flimsy Curtiss biplane from a temporary platform fitted to the bows of the cruiser USS *Birmingham*. On a later occasion some two months later, he made a deck-landing on a similar platform attached to the stern of the cruiser, *Pennsylvania*. The aircraft, equipped with several hooks, was brought to a halt within the limited distance available (the platform was only 120 feet long), by catching these hooks in arrester wires stretched across the platform, their ends weighted down by sand bags. This system, with, however, continual improvements, remained the basic method of landing aircraft on a carrier until the coming of Vertical Take-Off aircraft.

Ely's flights were carried out with the ships stationary in harbour, but it was soon realised

that a ship sailing into the wind gave an aircraft extra lift.

In 1913, Short Brothers produced the 'Short Folder'. Folding the wings of aeroplanes and seaplanes saved space, allowing more to be carried aboard ship.

Aerial Reconnaissance at sea

As early as 1903, navies throughout the world were searching for methods to see beyond the horizon; to spot enemy fleets before they came into view from the masthead. Experiments were carried out using giant kites towed behind fast ships, manned observation balloons, and airships fitted with Marconi's newly invented wireless; but to many, the obvious answer was the aeroplane.

Ships were adapted to carry seaplanes which could be lowered and cranked aboard by crane – these would become the eyes of the fleet, reporting an enemy's strength and disposition. By 1913 these seaplanes were able to transmit information to their mother ship. On 31 May, 1916, Seaplane 8359 made history. Lowered from *Engadine*, a Cross-Channel packet converted into a seaplane 'Carrier', she became the first aircraft to take part in a naval action.

At 15.30 hours, the Observer, Assistant Paymaster C. S. Trewin, RN, tapped out – 'Three enemy cruisers and five destroyers, distance 10 miles, bearing 9, steering course to the NW.' – then began the Battle of Jutland. Unfortunately, these 'carriers' could only operate in good weather, a relatively calm sea was necessary for the seaplanes to take-off and land.

The introduction of the compressed air catapult (the Americans first installed one on the quarterdeck of cruiser USS *Huntingdon* before World War I), enabled battleships and cruisers to carry their own observation aircraft.

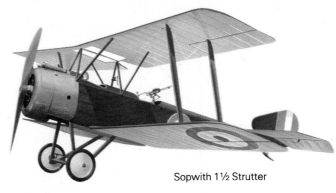

Sopwith 1½ Strutter

HMS *Argus*

Fairey 'Swordfish'

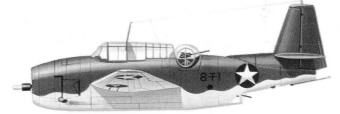

Grumman TBF – 1 'Avenger'

Mitsubishi A6M2 'Zero-Sen'

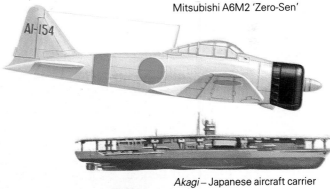

Akagi – Japanese aircraft carrier

'Seafire'

Rheinübung: Exercise Rhine

19.22 HOURS, 23rd May, 1941.

Kapitänleutnant Burkard von Mullenheim-Rechberg, Fourth Gunnery Officer of the battleship *Bismarck*, peering to starboard through his range director scanned the grey wastes of the Denmark Strait. From his position high in the after gunnery control tower of the 53,000 ton German battleship, he had a clear view of the pack ice hardly two kilometres away. The ship was zig-zagging to avoid ice flows – he swung the director to port – swirling fog patches, the occasional snow squall; beyond lay the minefields stretching to the coast of Iceland. The weather was perfect for eluding any British ships that might be searching for them in these northern waters.

The possibility of being sighted had haunted the ship's company ever since they had slipped out of Gotenhafen, in the Baltic, three days ago. Then, the ship's bandmaster had amazed the crew by striking up 'Muss i denn', a tune traditionally played only aboard battleships embarking on a long voyage. Later they had passed close by the Swedish aircraft-carrying cruiser, *Gotland*, as they went through the Kattegat – then a Spitfire had circled themselves and the heavy cruiser, *Prinz Eugen*, off Bergen. By now the Admiralty in London would know that a German task force was breaking out into the Atlantic to harry and destroy allied convoys carrying much needed supplies to Britain.

In fact, Major Tornborg, a top Swedish secret service officer, sympathetic to the Allied cause, had informed the British Naval Attaché of the *Gotland* sighting. This was later confirmed by Flying Officer Suckling from the cockpit of his Spitfire. German commerce raiders were breaking out. Hurriedly issued orders flew out from the British naval base at Scapa Flow; battleship *Prince of Wales* and the 'Mighty Hood', battlecruiser – terror of Kriegsmarine war

Battleship *Bismarck*

Statistics

Weight in metric tons: 1,000 kilogrammes to the ton
Weight: (net displacement), unloaded, 45,950 tons
Weight: fully loaded 50,950 tons
Length: 251 metres
Beam: 36 metres. *Bismarck* was wide in proportion to her length, this allowed her to have a more shallow draft for operations in shallow seas – North Sea etc.
Draft: fully loaded, 10.2 metres
Power: Electrical power was supplied by two diesel generators and six steam-driven turbo generators.

games – were to steam at full speed in a north-westerly direction. Heavy cruisers *Norfolk* and *Suffolk* patrolling the Denmark Strait were put on alert.

Grossadmiral Raeder's brilliant plan, code name Rheinübung, to send his capital ships into the Atlantic, depended very much on the element of surprise. Originally the task force was to have consisted of battleships *Bismarck*, *Gneisenau* and possibly *Bismarck*'s sister ship, *Tirpitz*; together with the heavy cruiser, *Prinz Eugen*. With the *Gneisenau* damaged and the *Tirpitz* not yet battle ready, Fleet Commander

Statistics of HMS *Hood*

Completed: 1920
Displacement: 42,000 tons
Fully loaded: 46,300 tons
Crew: 1,341–1419
Length: 860 feet
Beam: 105 feet 2 inches
Draught: 28 feet 3 inches
Armament: 8 × 15 inches; 12 × 5.5 inches; 8 × 4 inches AA guns; 5 × machine guns; 10 × Lewis guns; 4 × 21 inches torpedo tubes

Aircraft: 1
Armour: Barbettes, 12 inches; Main turrets, face – 15 inches; side – 12 inches; Director tower, 6 inches; Armoured belt, 12 inches

Some weights aboard Bismarck

Crew: 244 tons
Fuel oil: 8,700 tons, giving an operational range of 9,280 nautical miles, using approximately 44 tons an hour at 29 knots
Supplies: 194 tons – the cold storage space could hold 300 sides of beef and 500 pigs (dressed)
Water: 530 tons, drinking and washing

Total gunnery: 1,513 tons
Armour: 17,000 tons
Engines: 4,800 tons – 12 boilers drove 3 sets of turbines – (3 propellers) generated 150,000 horse-power, giving a top speed of 30 knots
Amount of paint to cover Bismarck: 220 tons
The Crew of Bismarck consisted of 103 officers, 1,962 petty officers and men
Prize crews, Admiral Lutjen's staff and war correspondents raised the number to 2,200.

German ships, well out of range of even *Bismarck*'s 38cm guns.

Through his headphones Mullenheim heard a report to Kapitän zur See Lindemann, *Bismarck*'s captain, 'Forward radar out of action'. As a result of jolting as the 38cm guns went off – they were blind forward, and could only rely on look-outs. Nothing seemed to be going right. The *Prinz Eugen*, her radar still intact took up position ahead of the *Bismarck*. Admiral Lütjens ordered full speed ahead, he had decided to shake off the shadowing cruisers. The bow waves rose as the German ships cut through the Arctic waters at close on 30 knots – through rain squalls, snow squalls; in and out of dense fog banks, behind smoke screens. At every clear patch, they looked astern – their shadows were always with them. Gradually it dawned on Lütjens that the British cruisers had an infinitely superior radar system to his own.

05.00 – 24 May – sunrise – brilliant clear weather.

Once again the alarm was sounding on the *Bismark* – the loudspeakers blared, 'Battle stations. Battle stations. Clear the decks for action'. Bulkhead doors slammed throughout the ship, thousands of trampling boots rang across the steel deck plates. Combat belts and gas masks were swiftly donned, hammers and life-jackets rolled in pouches. In each main turret, 64 men with pale sweaty faces waited to work the 38cm guns. 'Cleared for action' was reported to the Captain in the conning position from gun turrets, engine rooms and decks.

Two smoke trails appeared on the horizon ahead. Rapidly the ships closed to 30,000 metres. The *Bismarck*'s First Gunnery Officer, Korvettenkapitän Schneider, came over the fire control telephone, 'Two heavy cruisers ahead'. The 38cm turrets swivelled to bear on the target. The Second Gunnery Officer, Korvettenkapitän Albrecht thought they were too big for cruisers. When they opened up at 25,000 metres he was certain. His shout was deafening through the headphones, 'The *Hood*, it's the *HOOD*!'

At 05.55 Lindemann gave permission to fire. The *Bismarck*'s main armament roared out, aimed at the *Hood* and the *Prince of Wales*.

The *Bismarck*'s firing was devastating.

Lütjens was compelled to set out with only two raiders – a 'teaspoon' force he called it.

It was 19.22 hours. *Bismarck*'s alarm bell shrilled out, there was a 'contact' on the port bow. The radar and hydrophones had picked up a cruiser heading south-west at speed – it was *Suffolk*. An intercepted radio signal from *Suffolk* was rapidly decoded by the B-Dienst team – 'One battleship, one cruiser in sight at 20°. Range 7 nautical miles, course 240°.' The *Bismarck* had been spotted. A depressing start to Rheinübung. Who was the signal for? Was there a British fleet close to hand?

At 20.30 the Alarm bells shrilled again. Mullenheim swung his director round in time to catch a glimpse of a three-funnelled ship breaking from the fog – a heavy County class cruiser – *Norfolk*. Within forty seconds the *Bismarck*'s guns opened up; great columns of water were flung up around the cruiser, already laying down smoke as she made for the fog bank at full speed. The two British cruisers took up station astern of the

Six minutes and 93 rounds later it was all over. A heavy salvo made a direct hit; one 38 centimetre shell, piercing the *Hood*'s inadequate armour, went off in an after turret ammunition room, detonating more than 100 tons of explosive. Mullenheim saw a mountain of flame soar up between her masts, a main 15 inch turret cart-wheeled through the air, huge fragments of white-hot metal shot up from a pall of black smoke, the ship was one gigantic fireball. Three survived from a crew of 1419. In stunned silence the men of the *Bismarck* watched the *Hood* split in two and sink. Then they began to cheer, the 'Mighty *Hood*', pride of the Royal Navy was no more.

'The old "Black Devil's" done it this time.' Leutenant zur See Peters ignored the new Matrosenhauptgefreiter Moessmer's remark to his friend Bootsmannsmaat Melering. Officially no officer knew the lower deck nickname for the Fleet Commander. Efficient, but unpopular with those below him, Lütjens rarely discussed his decisions with subordinates, this led to differences of opinion between himself and his captain, Lindemann.

Later that day the messdeck chatter was silenced by the announcer of a German radio request programme. 'A request from the whole German Nation for the gallant crew of the *Bismarck* – "Come Back".' The strains of the sentimental popular song floated through the ship; on the crest of a wave the crew joined in.

During the action the *Prince of Wales* had suffered severe damage; one shell took away her bridge, wiping out everyone except Captain Leach and the Yeoman of Signals before she broke off the engagement. Lindemann urged Lütjens to give chase, but he refused. The *Bismarck* herself had received only three hits and no casualties, but one of these hits was serious. A shell had passed clean through the bows, causing *Bismarck* to ship 2,000 tons of sea water. She took on a list of 9° to port, her bows dipped 3°. It also ripped open a number of fuel tanks – 1,000 tons of oil were unusable. *Bismarck* was leaving a tell-tale trail of oil in her wake. Around midday Mullheim noticed the ship swing to the south – Lütjens had decided to run for St. Nazaire, 2,000 nautical miles away. The *Prinz Eugen* was ordered to continue into the Atlantic.

As they ran south they were still aware of the *Norfolk* and *Suffolk*, now accompanied by the damaged *Prince of Wales*, doggedly following astern. Lütjens was by now firmly convinced that nothing could shake them off. Deep in his heart he also knew that the British would throw in everything to avenge the sinking of the *Hood*. Only the complete destruction of the *Bismarck* would help erase the psychological harm Britain would suffer. He was right. There were now two other fleets hunting the *Bismarck*; from Scapa Flow, battleship *King George V*, battlecruiser *Repulse* and the aircraft carrier *Victorious*, ac-

Gunnery aboard the *Bismarck*

The main armament, the 38 centimetre guns, was mounted in four turrets – Anton and Bruno forward – Caesar and Dora aft. The 15 centimetre guns, mounted in 6 double turrets, were amidships on the upper deck. The surface fire control system could be operated from three armoured control stations – No. 1. forward, No. 2. in the Foretop – No. 3. – aft. Each of these stations could control the whole system if necessary (when both forward positions were knocked out, Mullenheim controlled what was left of the armament from the after station), should all the stations be knocked out, then the guns were directed by individual turret commanders. The forward and after control stations had three directors,

and the foretop station, four. These directors were basically powerful telescopes (only their upper lenses protruded above the armoured roof) used to measure bearings of enemy ships. The revolving cupolas above, housed optical range finders which together with the radar (the radar aerials were mounted on top of the cupola; German radar at the time had a shorter range than the optical equipment, was not as accurate and was sensitive to shock) measured the range of the target. Ranges and bearings were fed into two gunnery computer rooms, who in turn provided ballistic answers to the gunnery officers.

Inside the control station the gunnery officer would pass on

The *Hood* torn apart by the fearful explosion in her after turret ammunition room.

the instructions to the individual turrets and when the 'lock-ready-shoot' indicator showed a turret on target, a petty officer would press a button to fire. Guns could also be fired from the computer rooms or from the turrets themselves. Korvet-tankapitan Schneider used a 'bracketing group' system to land his shells on the target. A 'bracketing group' consisted of three salvos, fired so quickly that they were in the air at the same time, but aimed to land 400 metres apart. Once the target was straddled, the computer room calculated the correct range and bearing; the gunnery officer ordered 'Good rapid' and 'Firing for effect' began – either all eight guns or four gun salvos fore and aft.

Armament

Number of guns	Calibre	Range	Turret side	Armour front	Number of rounds per gun
8	38 cm	36,200 m	220 mm	320 mm	120
12	15 cm	23,000 m	40 mm	100 mm	150
16	10.5 AA	18,000 m	—	—	420
16	3.7 AA	—	—	—	2,000
12	2 cm AA	—	—	—	2,000

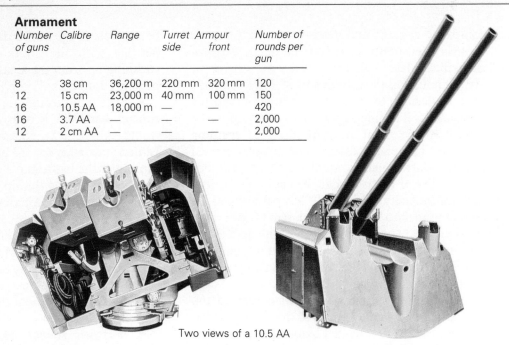

Two views of a 10.5 AA

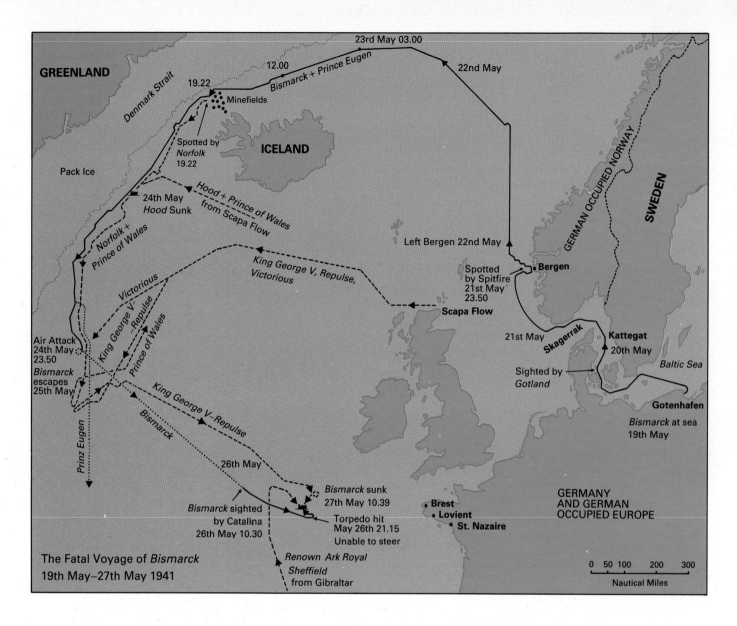

The Fatal Voyage of *Bismarck*
19th May–27th May 1941

companied by cruisers and destroyers. From Gibralter, battlecruiser *Renown*, aircraft carrier *Ark Royal* and a Sheffield class cruiser.

At 03.00 hours on the morning of 25 May, Lütjen's birthday, he decided to make one last attempt to throw off his shadows. Turning to starboard he completed a full circle, at one point going beyond the cruisers' radar sweep. The plan worked. The cruisers carried straight on. Unfortunately, so obsessed was Lütjens with the quality of British radar, he could not believe that he had actually shaken off his pursuers. This caused him to make a fatal error – he sent off two radio signals to the German Naval Group Command West in Paris during the forenoon of 25th May. It was enough. The British were able to take bearings and after several mistakes, finally computed his position. The Scapa Flow fleet changed course south, but it seemed too late. They were 150 miles north of the *Bismarck* and would never be able to catch her before she reached St. Nazaire. Admiral Tovey, commanding the British

fleets, was all too aware that his last hope of delaying her lay with the aircraft of the *Ark Royal*, now steaming up from the south. The *Bismarck* just had to be slowed down.

A 'buzz' ran through the *Bismarck*, they had broken contact with the British cruisers, spirits rose, they would soon be in St. Nazaire. At around noon Admiral Lütjens made his second blunder of the day. His voice came over the battleship's loudspeakers loud and cold. 'Seamen of the battleship Bismarck . . .', he praised them for a magnificent victory and then went on, 'We must die that Germany may live. At this hour we cannot think of our own fate. Whether we are killed is unimportant. The important thing is that we should sink one or more enemy ships.'

Without the slightest show of emotion, he concluded, 'At this moment there is only one watchword. Victory or Death.'

A horrified silence hung over the ship, morale plummetted, seamen looked at each other in fear; it really was all over, the Fleet Commander had said so. Kapitän zur See Lindemann's address an hour later helped, but it was not until twilight approached without incident that the crew's morale began to lift – they were racing towards St. Nazaire at 28 knots. Dawn of the 26th May found the crew jubilant – now only 690 miles from St. Nazaire.

Minutes later a big Allied flying boat broke through the low-lying cloud; soon she was signalling the *Bismarck*'s position. But it was only when the shadowing was taken over by a 'wheeled aircraft' that morale again began to fall. This could mean only one thing, there was an aircraft carrier in the vicinity.

The *Bismarck*'s aircraft alarm sounded at 2055 hours.

Through the Arctic twilight came 16 Swordfish, archaic 'Stringbags' that seemed to hover in the sky, but their 'eels' were deadly enough. They pressed home their attack with fanatical zeal – it was the last chance to stop the *Bismarck*. Miraculously the ship avoided being hit, equally miraculously so did the Swordfish – they all eventually returned to the *Ark Royal*.

The attack was all but over when two Swordfish came in from aft. At 20 metres, too low for his gun to bear on them, Matrosengefreiter Herzog saw the two torpedoes splash into the water. Seconds later came the violent explosion. *Bismarck* swung 12° to starboard in a circle, both rudders jammed, out of control, all steering gone. Every means was tried to steer her, but to no avail. Her circle brought the *Bismarck* on to a northern course directly approaching the oncoming enemy. At dawn of the 27th May Adolf Hitler's signal; 'I thank you in the name of the entire German people', did nothing to lighten the atmosphere of impending doom. Throughout the night the *Bismarck* was repeatedly harried by torpedo attack.

By 08.00 there was still no sign of the main units of the British fleet. Mullenheim realised that when they did come the *Bismarck* would have no chance against them. Yawling along at 7 knots, rudders stuck fast, it would be an execution, not a battle. Battleships *Rodney* and *King George V* appeared at 08.47 hours. They opened up at 20,000 metres, rapidly closing the range. Soon they were joined by the 8 inch batteries of the *Norfolk* and *Dorsetshire*. The badly yawling *Bismarck*, all but out of control, was helpless.

Matrosenstabsgefreiter Bruno Rzonca was one of a damage control party of five in compartment XI on the starboard side, at the start of the battle.

Hurrrrrrrrrumph – the first 16 inch shell landed on the port side, five seamen were killed. Acrid yellow smoke billowed through the compartment, stinking of sulphur and rubber, the heat was unbearable, but Rzonca hung on to the control centre telephone. A sudden blinding flash – a hell of noise, smoke and dust, the stench of scorching paintwork and Rzonca was alone – his mates all dead. He called up Central

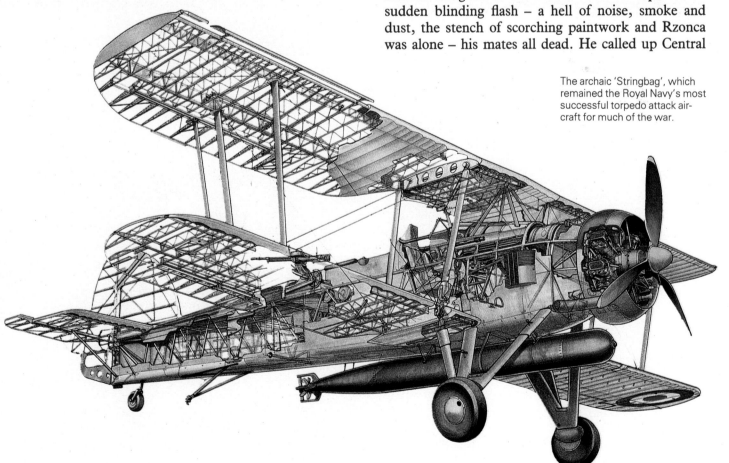

The archaic 'Stringbag', which remained the Royal Navy's most successful torpedo attack aircraft for much of the war.

71

'Yawling along at 7 knots, rudders
stuck fast, it would be an
execution, not a battle.'

Damage Control, but there was no answer. The flickering flames decided him, he staggered towards the watertight door, picking his way through smashed pipes and dangling wires.

Rzonca tried to calm a group of panic-stricken radio operators driven from their cabin by the flames and making for the aft dressing station. The dressing station itself was a shambles – men without arms, without legs; some sightless and screaming, others either cursing or praying. Surgeons and sick berth attendants swiftly moving from one stricken man to another, bandaging, consoling, giving morphia. A crash of a shell, the lights went out, water rushed in. Even in a few inches of water, those wounded unable to raise their heads, drowned. Another hit and those who could, scampered for the upper deck, Rzonca among them.

On the admiral's bridge, Günther Lütjens and his Chief of Staff, Kapitän zur See Netzbandt, searched the sky in vain for the promised Lüftwaffe squadrons. There was a rush of air, a flash of blinding light and the bridge was no more – Lütjens was among the first to die aboard the *Bismarck*.

Stepping over bodies strewn about the upper deck, Matrosenstabsgefreiter Penzlau, hearing the dreadful rush of air, threw himself to the deck. There were three violent explosions, one after the other, the screech of tortured metal, the whine of steel splinters ricochetting from the superstructure, the thud as they bit into the deck around him. He looked up to see smoke pouring from the forward 38 cm turret, Anton; its gun barrels pointed down. The forward gunnery

Control Armour

Forward Fire Control Station (In forward control post) 350 millimetres on the front face, 220 millimetres on top
Revolving dome: 200 millimetres
Foretop Control Station: 60 millimetres
After Fire Control Station: 150 millimetres
Revolving dome: 100 millimetres

The thickness of armour depended on the importance of the position to be armoured. *Bismarck* was divided into 22 watertight compartments. If a compartment became flooded, a compensating compartment was flooded to balance the ship. The ship's sides were covered with an armoured belt, ranging from 320 mm to 120 mm in thickness.

Decks

Upper deck: armoured along most of its length, 50 mm thick
Battery deck: 20 mm thick
Armoured deck: 110 mm 0 145 mm – 220 mm
Upper platform deck: 20 mm
Middle platform deck: 20 mm

Ship's Routine
Reveille: 06.00
Breakfast: 06.30–07.15, then
'Clean ship'
Muster for jobs: 08.00 – work,
maintenance, instruction and
battle practice
Noon break: 11.30–13.30, con-
tinue morning work
Evening meal: 17.00
Clean ship: 18.30
Swing Hammocks: 22.00

Crew of *Bismarck*
1 Kapitän zur See Lindemann
2 Petty Officer
3 Engineer
4 General ack-ack rating
5 Gunnery rating in 38 cm tunet
(anti-flash gear with gas mask)

control was smashed, men were screaming, trapped in the flames. Covering his ears he ran aft as far as 'Hindenberg Square', it was heaped with bodies one upon the other. Crouching behind them he waited for the end, it came quickly, a direct hit. The crew of an anti-aircraft gun saw the pile of corpses flung high into the air, among them Matrosenstabsgefreiter Penzlau.

In the after fire-control centre, Mullenheim was ordered to take over gunnery control.

'Action circuit aft', he called into the 'phone to the after computer room, he was answered by Leutnant zur See Aengeneyndt. Mullenheim had barely begun to issue his firing instructions when the director gave a violent shudder; a heavy shell had ploughed through the external antennae, a metre lower and it would have been 'kaput'. As it was, the control position was out of action – he ordered the rear turrets to fire independently. Unable to leave the control centre, a fire was raging outside, he and his two assistants had to sit it out. At last, at 10.00 they scrambled out to a scene of complete devastation. The anti-aircraft guns and searchlights surrounding the after station had disappeared. Gun turret Caesar, its barrels pointed high, was out of action; Dora, smoke-blackened, was a raging inferno, one barrel torn to shreds.

The last salvo from the *Bismarck* had been fired at 09.31. Mullenheim and his men made for the upper deck.

Lindemann's last order echoed throughout the *Bismarck*, 'Clear ship for scuttling.' In the forward dressing station Marinestabsarzt Arvid Thiele gave his instructions to the sick berth attendants, 'Get the wounded up top. Hurry.' He added, 'Leave those four in the corner'. Alone with the four hopeless cases he carefully filled a syringe with morphia and injected each man in turn; they drifted off, never to wake again.

Korvetten kapitän Junack was in the central control room when the order to prepare to scuttle came. He called, 'All hands on the upper deck', nodded to Obermaschinmaat Fischer and hastened up the ladder after his men. Fischer, responsible for detonating the demolition charges that would scuttle the ship, set the fuses; 120 seconds later there was a flash and a roar and water rushed into the turbine room.

On the upper deck, starboard side, Korvettenkapitän Nobis was directing the pitifully few survivors to abandon ship which was heeling over to port. The enemy had stopped firing. Unbelievably a 10 cm anti-aircraft gun opened up. Nobis shouted to the gunner to cease fire, but it was too late, the British began to fire again. He found himself somersaulting through the air, to hit the water with a resounding smack. Struggling to the surface, spitting oil and salt water, he looked back. The *Bismarck*, a battered smoking hulk, now completely on her side, slowly, slowly began to sink. Kapitän zur See Lindemann, standing on the forecastle, saluting, went down with her. The battle ensign still fluttered bravely.

The greatest battleship in the world – it had taken over fifty British warships to track her down and destroy her (2,876 shells and 39 torpedoes had been fired) was no more – the *Hood* had been avenged.

Of *Bismarck*'s crew of over 2,000, only 115 survived.

Lieutenant-Captain Luigi de la Penne, Alexandria, 1941

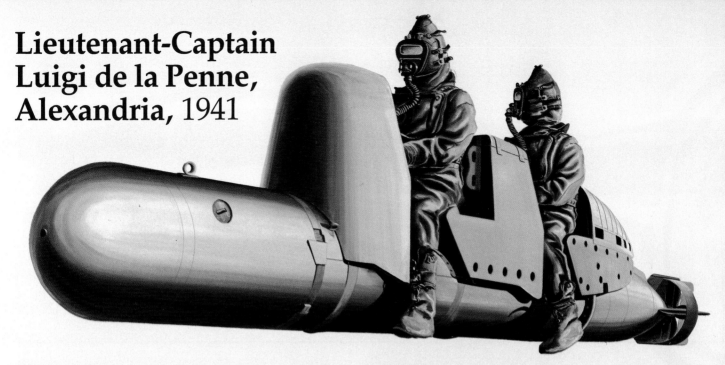

WATER foamed and bubbled from the *Scire*'s air vents as Captain Count Julio Borghese blew the air tanks of the Italian submarine and brought her gently to conning tower height. Nervously, he and the look-outs scanned through a 360 degree arc with their night binoculars – sound travels over water, someone ashore may have heard the roar of the escaping air. It was 20.00 hours on the night of 18 December, 1941 – a still, pitch-black night, with a calm sea lapping over the steel deck. It had been a nerve-wracking journey from Leros in Greece, constantly on the look-out for British destroyers; and that last eight kilometres through the minefields. Ruefully he thought about the return journey.

The enemy must surely know they were coming. Bitterly resentful, spying eyes continually watched the movements of Italian ships to and from their base at Leros, reporting them to the British. *Scire* was such a distinctive boat, who could miss the container tanks built into her deck? If *Scire* was out, it could mean only one thing – an attack on Alexandria. Borghese, staring through his glasses, could make out a faint lightening of the sky off the port bow – it had to be the British naval base, about 10 kilometres away. No Italian submarine had ever got this close before; two had tried, both had been lost with their entire crews. But Borghese's boat had had a lucky run. The Nile, in flood, muddying the sea for miles beyond its mouth, made detection from the air all but impossible – allowing the *Scire* to come in close; saving the attack group two or three hours in the water.

It was the attack group that now climbed from the conning tower to the deck, their rubber soles slapping against the iron rungs of the ladder. Six of them,

Statistics of the *Queen Elizabeth* and the *Valiant*

Queen Elizabeth: completed 1913 (see left)
Valiant: completed 1914
Displacement: 30,000 tons
Fully loaded: 35,000 tons
Crew: 1,124
Length: 643 feet
Beam: 104 feet
Draught: 30 feet
Speed: 25 knots
Armament: 8 × 15 inches; 8 × 6 inches; 5 × machine guns; 10 × Lewis guns.
Aircraft: 4
Armour: Main turrets, 11 inches
Armoured belt, above waterline – 6 inches
   at waterline – 13 inches
   below waterline – 8 inches
Below armoured belt, 6 inches × 4 inches

nightmare figures, heavily goggled and clad in rubberized canvas suits. Each wore a respirator face mask with a flexible rubber tube running to a bag strapped on their chest, below this was a metal cylinder filled with compressed pure oxygen – which was recycled – it allowed them to work at depths of up to 25 metres without a string of tell-tale bubbles escaping to the surface – but at that depth there was always a risk of blacking-out. Led by their group commander, 24 year-old, Lieutenant-Captain Luigi de la Penne, the Italian frogmen opened the container tanks and disconnected the leads charging the electric batteries of their 'maiali' (pigs) from the submarine. A wave to the conning tower and the *Scire* slipped under until the frogmen stood waist-deep in the sea. Hastily they dragged out three manned torpedoes and mounted astride them, the pilot in front, his diver behind him. They checked their equipment and started the electric motors; the only sound, a faint hum and the whirl of propeller blades.

It had all started back in the middle 30's, during the Abyssinian Campaign, when two marine engineer lieutenants, Tesei and Toschi, had built the first SLC – 'siluro a lunga corsa' – long-range torpedo; maiale– 'pig'. These human torpedoes, manned by two frogmen, were 5.5 metres long with a diameter of half-a-metre. Their almost silent electric motors drove them through the water at a speed of two knots, giving a range of 16 kilometres and a maximum working depth of 25 metres. Below 25 metres, the water pressure caused the thin metal of the maiali to buckle, rendering the torpedoes useless. The front section, a detachable warhead, was 1.40 metres long and contained 300 kilograms of high explosive, enough to tear through the keel of even the largest battleship. The main body of the maiali had diving tanks fore and aft, which, when filled with water to provide 'nil thrust', allowed them to travel just below the surface. A further tank, the 'crash-diving' tank operated by a lever, enabled it to submerge as it was flooded. The pilot (seated behind a protective housing) steered by means of a control column, which also operated the diving rudders and horizontal-plane rudders. Set into the dashboard in front of him was a magnetic compass depth gauge and ammeter. His diver sat to the rear, forward of the motor and tool box, containing such equipment as compressed air net-cutters, clamps and a compressed-air net-lifter.

Luigi de la Penne, who had always had a passion for submarines, was considered too young to command one, so, early on he volunteered for the Small Weapons Unit of the Italian Navy. Here, together with a number of other dare-devil frogmen (these were eventually whittled down to ten in number), he was trained to operate a manned torpedo. Months were spent in learning to navigate them over long distances

– day and night – penetrating anti-submarine nets and making dummy attacks on ships in harbour. At the outbreak of war, the attacks becoming real, he met with varying success. The young Lieutenant-Captain himself had already gained a reputation, but he had recently lost a maiali in an unsuccessful attack and was fiercely eager to really prove himself. This time it would be another matter; he would lead his attack force into Alexandria harbour and sink two of Britain's remaining three battleships in the Mediterranean, HMS *Valiant* and HMS *Queen Elizabeth* (he did not know that the third, HMS *Barham*, had already been sunk by a German U-boat).

The whine of the *Scire*'s electric motors grew louder, Captain Borghese was anxious to be off. A hushed 'Good luck', the muffled thud of the conning tower hatch, water foaming along the submarine's sides and she was diving – bows pointing towards the open sea. Tomorrow night she would rendezvous off Rosetta to pick them up – with any luck. Linked together by a cable, with only their heads above water, the pilots turned their craft towards Alexandria. This was the moment they had rehearsed over and over again, using a detailed model of the British base to guide them. Each knew their target, each knew exactly where it lay in the harbour – Italian Intelligence had seen to that. De la Penne and his diver, Leading-Seaman Emilio Bianchi, were to sink *Valiant*; Captain Antonio Marceglia and Leading-Seaman Spartaco Schergat had *Queen Elizabeth* as their target. Captain Vincenzo Martelotta, with his diver, Mario Marino, were to attack an unknown aircraft carrier – should it be there; if not, there was a fully-laden oil tanker; they carried bombs to ignite any fuel that might spill out from the ruptured oil tanks.

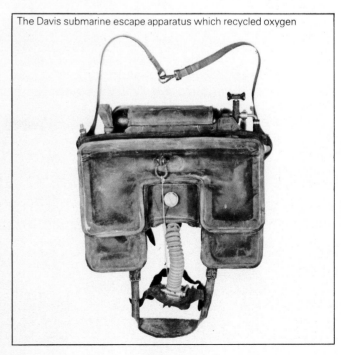

The Davis submarine escape apparatus which recycled oxygen

Travelling at 2 knots, only centimetres apart, they headed for the enemy base, chatting together in whispers to keep up their spirits. Two endless hours passed, as they crawled slowly towards their objective – de la Penne diving now and then to measure the depth of the water to check if they were still on course. Suddenly the beam of the lighthouse at Ras-al-Tin came on, sweeping across the water dead ahead. As the first shock wore off, they realised that with only their heads showing, there was little chance of them being seen from the jetty. It was bitterly cold and with water seeping through holes in his suit, de la Penne began to shake – he wondered if it was the cold alone that was responsible. Many considered their mission imposs-ible, he had grave doubts himself, but he was deter-mined to go on at all costs. To go on and strive somehow to balance the crippling losses inflicted on his country's navy by the British at Taranto and Matapan. He signalled his team to stop, rest and eat. Wolfishly they gobbled down the provisions carried in waterproof containers – they had worked up an appetite since leaving the submarine.

Once more they started up their motors and fol-lowed the jetty towards the harbour entrance, a hundred metres out to avoid a belt of remote-con-trolled acoustic mines. An hour later, de la Penne, soaked to the skin, his teeth chattering with cold, heard a sharp crack. Three minutes later there was another, a further three minutes, then another, but this time much louder. In the distance, slowly closing, he could dimly make out a foaming phosphorescent bow wave coming directly towards them. What bad luck, having got this far, to run into a guard boat. The crew were lobbing 10 kilo bombs over the side at regular intervals, on the chance of destroying any frogmen in the vicinity. He knew what an underwater explosion, even from a small 10 kilo bomb, could do to the human body, it had over twice the force in water that it had on land. Cold forgotten, tight with anger, he ordered his team to don face masks and stand by to dive. But already it looked too late, the next bomb exploded 30 metres away, he felt the shock wave carry through the water, the maiali reared dangerously. The next one must finish them off; most probably, explod-ing the warheads, it would hurl both them and the guard boat sky high. He huddled forward over the controls, eyes shut, knuckles white on the steering column. When the explosion came it seemed further away, he opened his eyes, the boat had turned before releasing its final bomb and was moving off into the distance.

Although shaken, tired and numb with cold after four to five hours in the water, they set course for the anti-submarine boom, three lines of steel nets, each weighing several tons. The pilots could hardly ma-noeuvre their craft for the cold. Then down, down

through the murky water, searching for gaps in the heavy steel netting – there were none. The group commander hesitated to use the compressed air net-cutters, what if the nets were wired for sound? Even if not, an alert operator might pick up the noisy cutters on his sonar equipment. Surfacing, they tried to swim their chariots over the nets – they were too high. On the stroke of midnight, as if by magic, the lights went on that illuminated the sandbanks and marked the deep channel into Alexandria harbour. The starboard boom ship chugged across the channel dragging open the heavy nets. Hooting, four graceful destroyers, making no more than four or five knots, slipped into the deep channel – the Italians alongside them, a metre or so from their hulls. Pushed under by the destroyers' wash, the frogmen came up choking and spitting sea water, there was no question of wearing their masks, reflections from the goggles would be a certain give away.

At last they were in. The commander gave the signal for liberty of manoeuvre; the group split up for attack. It was easy to spot the *Valiant*, a number of merchant ships were unloading beneath bright, quayside lights. The battleship lay little more than a kilometre away, her vast black bulk silhouetted against the gloom. Apart from the quayside activity, the harbour was still, they could hardly believe their luck – they had not been expected at all. A gentle half-hour's cruise through the oily, litter-strewn water, past the stern of an old French battleship, *Lorraine*, and they were within a hundred metres of their target. It was there that they ran into *Valiant*'s anti-submarine net, a curious rope affair lined with steel balls, 20 centimetres in diameter, arranged close to each other, which set up a raucous clatter with the harbour swell. Manhandling the maiali over the steel balls caused a fearful racket; de la Penne and Bianchi broke into a sweat despite the cold. At last they were over, and although they could clearly see the glow of a cigarette on the upper deck of the battleship, there was, miraculously, no general alarm.

The commander took his bearing on the centre of *Valiant*, submerged and headed straight for her at a depth of five to six metres. In total darkness, they dare not use their torches, the only sound the faint hum from their motors, they edged forward towards the ship's keel. A sudden black shape loomed up, they hit the hull of the battleship with a sickening, dull thud – surely they must hear that aboard? The maiale, flooding, began to sink, frantically de la Penne fought to turn off the motor, but his hands were stiff with cold – he failed. The other diver had already kicked away from his seat and was searching for the rolling chock on the port side of the battleship to secure the first clamp. After attaching a wire to the warhead, he would swim under the battleship to secure the second clamp to the starboard rolling chock.

The maiale dropped 17 metres to the bottom, spun round, then ploughed on, until it finally stopped dead, its propellers choked by the slimy ooze. De la Penne, by now chest-deep in the liquid mud of the harbour

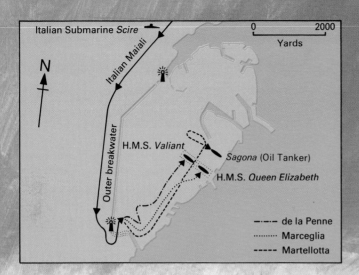

bed, was becoming desperate. Despairingly he peered through the murky gloom, calling on Bianchi to try to free the propeller – no answer. He swam to the stern of the maiale, there was no sign of the other man, he must have fainted and floated to the surface. Deciding he must find Bianchi before he gave their presence away, he replenished his respirator from the oxygen cylinders, kicked clear of the mud and swam upwards, unwinding his 'elevator' as he went. (The elevator was a thin cord wound round a piece of wood, with one end attached to the maiale, this allowed him to find his way back.)

Four metres from the surface the water became much lighter; his head broke water, directly in the beam of a searchlight. A swift look round, there was no sign of Bianchi, but the battleship was as quiet as the grave, *Valiant* had not been alerted to the attack. He slipped under and swam down to the torpedo, now almost hidden in the mud, he found that a steel cable had wrapped itself round the propeller, it was stuck fast. Frantically he grappled with it, struggling to manoeuvre the warhead to a position below the centre of the ship. A cloud of mud rose up; with a squelch the maiale broke free and moved, only a centimetre, but it moved. Encouraged by this, de la Penne, guided by the thud of the ship's pumps, dragged it centimetre at a time towards *Valiant*. Heart pounding with the effort, blinded by the sweat pouring down his face, he paused to clear his mask. In his attempt to wipe the mask clear it became filled with water, he could neither see nor breathe – there was nothing else for it, be began to gulp down the foul-tasting harbour water.

Feeling sick and thirsty, the diver surfaced for fresh air; it was quiet and still, they had still not been discovered. Down again, he was once more dragging the warhead towards the thud of the pumps. After forty minutes of agonising toil, it lay under the centre of *Valiant*'s keel, directly below an ammunition locker. There was a wild drumming in his ears, he felt faint and dizzy, he could scarcely breathe; but he managed to set the time fuse and cover the glowing instrument panel with mud. The warhead would go up in three hours time. His knees buckled, it became suddenly darker, he passed out.

De la Penne awoke to the sound of rifle fire. Bullets were spurting the water around him as he floated helplessly, only metres from the side of *Valiant*. Finally alerted, her crew were now lining the rail, pouring volley after haphazard volley at the Italian frogman. Mindlessly kicking his flippers, he made for the fore buoy and crouched behind it – unhit. He looked up, there was Bianchi huddled astride the buoy, clinging to the ship's hawser. A searchlight flooded across them and minutes later a ship's boat came alongside. The frogmen, roughly prodded with rifles, were hustled aboard and taken to *Valiant*, where the officer of the watch, mistaking them for parachutists, sent them ashore to be interrogated at Ras-al-Tin lighthouse. Here they were stripped of their sub-aqua gear, down to their uniform overalls – at least they would not be shot as spies. Bianchi, who was questioned first, shook his head at de la Penne as he came out of the interrogation, he had obviously told them nothing.

'So we've finally got de la Penne' – his interviewer was Commander Crabbe. Himself a renowned frogman, he was to disappear many years later whilst diving beneath a brand new Russian cruiser in Portsmouth harbour. The Englishman sat idly spinning a cowboy six-shooter. 'I am Lieutenant-Captain Luigi de la Penne of the Italian Royal Navy and more than that I cannot tell you.'

'Don't worry', laughed the Commander, 'I'll find a way to make you talk' – he did.

The two Italians were taken back aboard *Valiant* and closely questioned by the ship's commander, Captain Morgan, with the same result – name, rank and number only. To their horror they were hurried

below to an ammunition locker, where they were guarded by pale-faced British sailors – only de la Penne knew that the magazine was directly above the fused warhead. Time was ticking away; it was well past 04.00 hours, the explosive charge was due to go off at 06.00 hours. The Italians gratefully gulped down rum and lit up cigarettes offered by the British sailors – a fiery glow spread through them as the spirit went down, they were still blue with cold. Bianchi, who had no idea where the warhead lay, dropped off to sleep – he had always been a cool one. There was no sleep for de la Penne – he was too much aware of the bomb ticking away beneath his feet. He glanced at the young sailors, they were only obeying orders, he couldn't let them go up with him. One of them held out a packet of Players to him, he noticed the time on the lad's wrist watch, 05.45 hours – fifteen minutes to go. He came to a decision.

'Take me to Captain Morgan.'

'Captain, look, your ship will be going sky-high in a few minutes from now and there's nothing you can do about it, get the crew to safety, if you've a mind to do so.'

But, refusing to reveal the position of the warhead, he was taken below once more to the ammunition locker – he could hear the Tannoy blaring out – 'Stand by to abandon ship. Stand by to abandon ship.' As the magazine hatch slammed shut above his head, he turned to Bianchi, 'Pray to God, because now there's nothing more to be done for us.' But Bianchi had gone – he was completely alone. In an agony of suspense and fear he began to pray very quickly – why this injustice? Why this torture? He was still praying when the flash came – a deafening roar – then nothing. He regained consciousness to the choking smell of high explosive fumes, water was cascading into the compartment, mercifully the magazine hatch had been blown off. With the water already surging round his waist, he scrambled up the ladder, heedless of a sharp pain in his knee, covered in blood. The scene on the upper deck was one of panic; men were running aimlessly about, officers were shouting orders, their voices lost in the general hubbub. De la Penne made his way aft; he was astonished when a number of *Valiant*'s sailors saluted him, it could only be the gold bars on his shoulders. The sun was coming up behind *Queen Elizabeth*, moored 500 metres ahead, it was going to be a stunningly beautiful day – he was happy to be alive – it had been a miracle.

As he watched, *Queen Elizabeth* lifted out of the water, there was a flash and a violent roar as the sound raced at them across the water. So Marceglia and Schergat had succeeded. At that moment, Marceglia was steering his maiale towards a deserted quay in the old trading port of Alexandria, pin-pointed by Intelligence. Hurrying up the ancient, slime-covered stone steps, they threaded their way through the old town, eventually reaching Rosetta, their rendezvous point. It was there that Italian Intelligence let them down. The two frogmen were arrested trying to cash the British banknotes with which they had been provided – these were invalid in Egypt.

The third team, Marlotta and Marino, had left their warhead dangling below the stern of the 7,750 ton *Sagona*, an oil tanker. But by now the alarm had been raised; ships were weighing anchor and making for the open sea. Destroyers, hooting wildly, were dashing about, sweeping the water with their searchlights. The two frogmen were picked up by a waiting naval patrol as they crawled, exhausted, up the steps of the old pier. Aboard *Valiant*, de la Penne felt the ship slowly listing, *Queen Elizabeth* had already settled on the bottom, her upper deck a foot or two above the water. Four degrees, five, six degrees – she was going to capsize – then, to the bitter disappointment of Lieutenant-Captain de la Penne, she stopped and slowly settled on the bottom.

The following day *Scire* waited in vain off Rosetta, Captain Borghese stayed as long as possible, then he reluctantly submerged, setting course for Leros. The daring men of the Italian Small Weapons Unit were being closely interrogated before being shipped off to a Prisoner of War camp in Palestine. But they had put Britain's two remaining battleships in the Mediterranean out of commission for many months to come, they had avenged Taranto and Matapan.

___

Human torpedoes and midget submarines

As early as World War I, the Italian Navy began to experiment in the use of midget submarines and other underwater assault methods to penetrate enemy naval bases unseen. By World War II they had perfected highly successful techniques, relying mainly on manned torpedoes, 'maiali' and frogmen. The maiale, more a slow-moving underwater vehicle with a detachable warhead than a torpedo, was nevertheless nicknamed 'human torpedo' by the British. Later in the war the Royal Navy produced its own successful 'Chariot', a direct copy of the maiale. Attempts to use the 'Chariot' in northern waters ended in failure, the bitterly cold seas proving too much for the pilots – it was then restricted to use in the Mediterranean only.

In the main, both Britain and Germany concentrated on the production of midget submarines, launched close to their targets by parent submarines. By 1943, the Royal Navy had commissioned a number of 'X-craft' four-man midget submarines, designed to penetrate Norwegian fjords to attack enemy warships, notably, *Tirpitz*. Unlike the German midgets (German 'K-craft' were used chiefly to hold up the expected invasion of the European continent, but with little success), the 'X-craft' carried no torpedoes, relying on two ½ ton high explosive side charges, which they released beneath their target.

Human torpedoes, first used by the Japanese during the Russo-Japanese War of 1904, were re-introduced in the closing stages of World War II when things were going badly for them. Known as 'Kaiten' (Heaven Shakers) they became part of the suicidal 'Special Attack Corps', along with the 'Kamikaze' (Divine Wind) suicide aircraft. By including an extra section between the 3,000lb warhead and the oxygen motor of a giant 'Long, Lance' torpedo, the Japanese provided a pilot's compartment – cramped even for a small man. Launched from below the surface by a large 'I' class submarine, the kaiten, fitted with a stubby periscope and a set of controls enabling its pilot to direct the torpedo run, could travel over 14 miles at a speed of 30 knots. The pilot was given a course, speed and length of running time before leaving the mother submarine. This in theory would bring him within 500 yards of his target, when he would raise his periscope, adjust his course and make a suicide dash for the enemy at over 40 knots. However, in practice only a handful of ships were sunk for the loss of eight 'I' class submarines and most of the kaiten put into service.

X-Craft

British
'X-Craft'
Statistics
Crew: 4
Displacement: 27 tons
Armament: 2 × ½ ton high explosive side-charges
Speed: surfaced, 6½ knots; submerged, 5½ knots

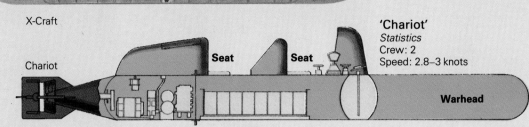

Chariot

Seat   **Seat**

Warhead

'Chariot'
Statistics
Crew: 2
Speed: 2.8–3 knots

German
'Seehund'
Statistics
Crew: 2
Displacement: 15 tons
Armament: 2 × 21 inch torpedoes
Speed: surface, 7¾ knots; submerged, 6 knots

Seehund

'Marder'
One man torpedo.

'Biber'
Crewed by one man, this midget submarine carried two torpedoes.

Japanese
'Kaiten'
Statistics
Crew: 1
Warhead: 3,000 pounds high explosive.
Range: over 14 miles.

Speed: cruising, 30 knots; maximum, over 40 knots.
Length: nearly 30 feet.

'Kairyu'
Statistics
Crew: 2
Armament: 2 × 18 inches torpedoes. Later, when used in suicide missions, the torpedoes were replaced by a 1,000 pound

high explosive warhead
Displacement: 46 tons.
Speed: surfaced 23 knots; submerged 19 knots.

Kairyu

Kaiten

Commander Paul Bootherstone, HMS *Arrow*, 1982

10.50 GMT, Sunday, 23 May, 1982.

In the half-light of a Falkland's dawn, the convoy slipped into San Carlos Water; it looked like being a calm, clear, possibly sunny day. Ideal conditions for an Argentine air attack. They needed good weather and flying conditions – both at their end and over the Falklands – for refuelling, selecting their target and making their run-in. But despite refuelling in the air, they were at the extremity of their range allowing only 4 or 5 minutes combat time over the target. A 15 knot wind barely rippled the surface of the Bay which remained calm in all but the roughest weather. That had been a major consideration in choosing it for the British beach-head in retaking the Falklands; that and its geographical position. Lying at the western end of the main island, it was a narrow strip of water surrounded by a defensive screen of hills which offered maximum protection against air attack. Argentine pilots, sweeping over the hill tops, would have just seconds in which to choose a target and make their bombing run.

The supply ships, grouping off the eastern shore of San Carlos Water, had no sooner dropped anchor than helicopters began ferrying men, machinery and equipment to the beach-head. A Wessex V made for the shore, a sedately swinging Land Rover slung beneath it. Another flew in with more Rapier missile equipment to strengthen the anti-aircraft batteries ashore. A third 'helo' was loaded with ammunition. They were

all careful to remain low to avoid detection; 'map of the earth' flying; hugging the contours of the ground. The escort ships, frigates and destroyers, positioned themselves around the merchantmen, ready to throw up an anti-aircraft umbrella of crossing fire in the event of an 'Argie' air attack.

Commander Paul Bootherstone, captain of a Type 21 frigate, HMS *Arrow*, choosing his position carefully, took his ship as close to the beach as possible, short of running her aground. Nestling beneath a steep cliff, the *Arrow* had only 180 degrees of attack to defend. Completely protected from the east, she would be able to concentrate on Argie aircraft coming in from the west and ahead or astern down the length of the water – looking for all the world like a Scottish loch. He was also careful to position the ship out of sight of an Argie observation post, perched on top of a distant mountain.

Paul Bootherstone, a career officer, joining the Royal Navy at the age of sixteen, had decided to specialise in aviation. Since then his experience had been wide and varying. A pilot flying Gannets from HMS *Hermes*, commander of an RAF training squadron, captain of a mine hunter, XO (First Lieutenant) of a Type 21 class frigate, a spell responsible for pilot recruiting and training at the Ministry of Defence and since October 1981 captain of *Arrow*. He looked round from the bridge at his bustling ship, the crew preparing for the expected air attacks; yes, this was without

HMS *Arrow*

Specifications
Type 21, General purpose
frigate
Pennant Number: F173
Completed: 1975
Displacement: 2,815 tons
Length: 384 feet
Beam: 41.7 feet
Complement: 171; 11 officers;
160 ratings
Engines: 2 × Rolls-Royce Olym-
pus TM3, gas turbines, speed
over 30 knots; 2 × Rolls-Royce
Tyne RB 209 for cruising. Range
30 knots – 1,200 miles; 17 knots
– 4,000 miles

Principal armament:
1 × 4.5 inch Vickers Mark 8
automatic gun
Exocet missiles: surface-to-surface
Seacat missiles: surface-to-air,
surface-to-surface
2 × triple anti-submarine tubes
1 × Westland Lynx multi-purpose helicopter
Crew: pilot, observer
Length: 49 feet
Speed: 160 knots
Engine: Rolls-Royce Gem
2 × 20 millimetre Oerlikon guns
Running cost in 1976 – £3.3
million per ship per year – not
including helicopter

Arrow, a general purpose frigate, was designed to protect
convoys and other naval forces
against attack by surface ships
and submarines, using surface-
to-surface guided missiles – Ex-
ocets and anti-submarine tor-

pedoes fired from 2 triple torpedo tubes on her upper deck.
By use of Seacat surface-to-air
guided missiles, fired from a
quadruple launcher, she is fully
able to defend herself against
aircraft, missiles or fast patrol
boats. Her multi-purpose
Westland Lynx, highly effective in an anti-submarine role
and to search and strike against
surface vessels, can carry either
6 air-to-surface guided missiles,
or 2 anti-submarine torpedoes.
Fully computerised, highly
automated weapon systems,
sophisticated action information equipment, a centralised
storeroom complex supplying
replaceable parts by vertical
hoist and easily operated gas-
turbine engines, have enabled
the normal complement of a
ship of this size to be reduced
by two thirds to 171. This has
allowed more space for the
ship's company accommo-
dation which paid off during
the Falklands campaign, when
they were continuously at sea
for over 100 days. *Arrow* has
separate dining halls for both
senior and junior ratings, a
laundry, sick bay and com-
prehensive recreational facili-
ties, including, television,
video, a library, radio and
cinema.

doubt the most satisfying part of his career to date. He
ran a tight ship, the morale and efficiency were high,
the crew capable of facing anything that was likely to
come, despite the fact that the average age was just 21.
It never ceased to amaze him that 18 and 19 year olds
could be so coolly efficient.

His eye ran over the sleek lines of *Arrow*, the sharp,
elegant sweep of her bow, her compact superstructure,
the squat, raked funnel, the never idle 'helo' pad at the
stern. A good ship, one that could match any compar-
able warship in the world – a worthy member of the
'Fighting Fourth' squadron.

A watery sun peeped out at 11.30 hours 'Zulu
Time', it was clear, but bitterly cold. From the
beginning it was decided that the Fleet should keep
'Zulu Time', Greenwich Mean Time and gradually the
crews' 'body clocks' had adjusted themselves to an
unnatural time sequence; here at the Falklands they
were three hours ahead of the 'Argies'. The ships'

companies had already breakfasted and cleaned ship well before dawn, and more important, they had got over that 'lowest ebb' which comes around six in the morning and were now fully alert and ready for action. The captain scanned the further shore through his binoculars, sheep and cattle were grazing in the rolling pastures, an early farmer was driving his tractor across a field. They would be coming any minute now. He made for the Ops. room (Operations room) below the upper deck, directly under the bridge. On the way he passed crew members closed up at action stations (the whole ship's company stood to for the duration of action stations), waiting, quietly confident, for the Argentine attacks they knew to be inevitable. They had sharpened up well since 2 April, when the signal directing the Flag Officer First Flotilla to proceed south with a number of the exercise ships had been received.

It was then they had been informed that the Argentines had invaded the Falklands – it had seemed inconceivable. Phase I of the Navy Springtrain completed, the Fleet had sailed out into the Atlantic from Gibraltar, to continue Phase II of the exercise. Im-mediately, the eight ships detailed to head for the Falklands, paired off with those returning home, to relieve them of their spare stores and gear, by jackstay, boat and vertrep (Vertical Replenishment – by helicopter). Every type of naval and victualling stores, missiles, torpedoes, electrical spares and ammunition was transferred to the Advance Group. (*Arrow* – 21 type frigate; *Brilliant* – 22 type frigate; six Guided Missile Destroyers, *Sheffield*, *Coventry*, *Antrim*, *Glamorgan*, *Plymouth* and *Glasgow*. In all, seven frigates of the 'Fighting Fourth' eventually found their way to the Falklands – the eighth was in the Far East.) They turned south into the Atlantic swell in brilliant sunshine, still at cruising stations, six hours on, eighteen hours off. War seemed remote and unbeliev-able.

Yet the unbelievable had happened. The captain realised that he had to convince the crew that this was

for real. Regardless of the fact that technically the two countries were not at war, unless the Argentines quit the Falklands the Fleet would open up hostilities when it arrived. A hastily prepared presentation with photographs, drawings, maps and statistics was put together and broadcast over the ship's close circuit TV system. Main points were emphasised – why the Falklands were British – what had happened, what was happening, what was likely to happen – the time it would take to get there. Under the warm southern sun, the ship cut through the Atlantic at speed, the crew continually exercising and drilling for the action that seemed likely to come. White-haired, but young, Lieutenant Len Bamber, the Supply Officer, in his second role as Flight Deck Officer, put the flight deck through its paces. By the time *Arrow* reached the South Atlantic she was battle ready. Extra ammunition had been taken on, dumps of emergency food stocks and medical supplies were set up in strategic positions around the ship, the men honed to combat readiness. 'Crossing the Line' went almost unnoticed – the traditional ceremony would have to come later.

Their first gale had blown up south of Ascension Island at 20 degrees of latitude. Vast 30 feet waves had crashed over *Arrow*, hurling spray beyond the bridge,

as she ploughed through the rollers. Her stabilizers helped neutralize the roll, but there was a sickening pitch as her bows fell with a smack into the trough of a wave, but by then the ship's company had found their 'sea legs' and even the half dozen who were notoriously seasick, ceased to be effected. Prior to that it had taken guts and determination to continue manning their stations – but they did. Oddly enough by week three everyone on board, without exception, was completely cured of seasickness for the rest of the operation. The gale lasted two days, the crew's first introduction to the dreadful seas that occur in the South Atlantic. The weather conditions could change dramatically, literally within the hour. Early one morning a Merchant Navy tanker came alongside to replenish *Arrow*. The oil pipes were run out under clear skies with a 15 knot wind blowing from the north. An hour and a half later – they had barely finished oiling – it had veered round to the south and a 50 knot gale was lashing the sea into a fury.

Reminiscent of HMS *Victory*'s preparation before Trafalgar, *Arrow* had already stored all her trophies, furnishings, mirrors and excess furniture in the bowels of the ship. She was ready to go to war.

When the Advance Group reached 40 degrees of latitude, the edge of the 'Roaring Forties', they began 'Box sailing' in gigantic squares, as they waited for the aircraft carriers *Invincible* and *Hermes*, with the rest of the main force, to catch up. Destroyers *Plymouth* and *Antrim* went off to assist the group retaking South Georgia. As it became colder, the crew were urged to put on layers of clothes – hill-climbing fashion. To ensure they did, the heating was turned off throughout the ship – by tradition seamen hate wearing a lot of clothing. (Layers of clothing help keep the body temperature up should they be forced to jump into a sub-zero temperature sea.) As luck would have it the *Arrow* had cruised in the Arctic Ocean under similar conditions the previous year, so most of the crew were only too aware of the need for adequate clothing.

Dressed for the weather many of them made a comic sight. 'Long Johns' – woollen combinations – were worn under No. 8's, blue jean trousers and shirt; over this went layer upon layer of jerseys. Overall they wore foul weather tops and trousers tucked into thick sea boot stockings and sea boots. This was topped by a woollen Balaclava or cap. The foul weather gear was replaced at an early stage by green cotton overalls – flown out from the UK. They came in three sizes, gross – grosser – grossest, the smallest size being too big for the six feet odd Commander. They were later replaced by smaller sizes, but not before Leading Steward Walters, all 5'2" of him, had presented himself to Paul Bootherstone, his overalls ballooning round him; sleeves dangling inches below his hands, trouser bottoms concertina-like round his feet.

The food aboard *Arrow* had been good throughout, but at one point the galley ran out of potatoes and bread-making flour, the chief cook and his mates were forced to turn to rice as a substitute. The crew began to 'drip' about 'Chinky nosh', much to the delight of Tao Lin Bo, the 'Number 1 Chinese Boy', the 'Dhobie man'. Tao ran the ship's laundry as a private enterprise, he was neither Navy, nor an official member of the ship's company. Each of the other ships had a fellow countryman of Tao's offering a similar service.

At last the *Hermes'* Group arrived, the monotonous cruising ceased, they had been at defence stations (six hours on six hours off) ever since leaving Ascension Island. The combined fleet immediately entered the 200 mile Total Exclusion Zone (TEZ). The action was on. On 4 May, the destroyer *Sheffield*, hit amidships by an Exocet missile, was soon a mass of flames – an Entendard aircraft had fired it at a range of 20 miles, unseen beyond the horizon. Ignoring the risk of further explosions, *Arrow* went alongside to help fight the raging fires – a shuttle of 'helos' flew off the injured. Sadly the order had been given to abandon ship, the fire was beyond control, and the crew were swiftly transferred to *Arrow*.

Midday of the 23 May came with still no sign of the 'Argies'. The midday meal was brought to the men at their action stations. Leading Steward Walters handed the Captain his at his position at the centre of the Ops. room – a bowl of stew and a great hunk of bread. It had a different name to yesterday's stew, yet it tasted the same – but it was hot and very good, living up to the high standard set aboard *Arrow*. With a grin he remembered that most of the meat in their cold room was Argentinian. His stew finished, the Captain

glanced round the Ops. room, pitch dark but for the flickering lights on the instrument panels, the lighted edges of the perspex stake boards and the constant orange sweep of the radar at the six displays. The dim figure of Lieutenant Commander Churton, Principal Weapons Officer (Underwater), ghostly in anti-flash gear, moved about in the gloom, his microphone on a long lead. There was the squeak of chinagraph pencils and the ping of sonar equipment. They were a good team, very much aware that the very life of the ship depended on their accuracy, as they sat, eyes glued to their displays, occasionally tapping information into their computer keyboard at the side of each table.

Through his left headphone, the Captain could hear the chatter of radio information from the Army observation posts ashore and the radar picket ship in the centre of San Carlos Water. This was the closest early warning of 'Argie' attacks he was likely to receive – the surrounding hills rendered the detection of low-flying aircraft highly improbable. Internal information

Cutaway of the 4.5 inch, computerised and fully automatic main gunnery armament of HMS *Arrow*.

RIGHT: Commander Paul Bootherstone and his steward. The green cotton overalls came in three different sizes gross, grosser, and grossest.

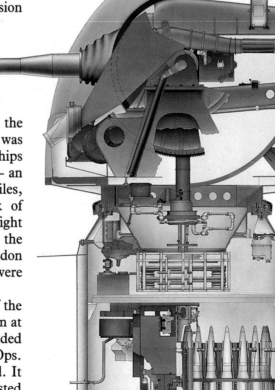

from the Ops. room and the rest of the ship came through his right headphone – information from the radar and sonar positions. Chief Petty Officer (Radar) Boyle, Gun Director Blind, realised only too well that he and Petty Officer (Radar) McDonald would be in the hot seat during the forthcoming air attacks – there was little likelihood of attack by surface ships or submarines. Leading Seaman Jury was already hard at it sorting out the 'helo' tracks on his display. 'Helo' traffic was in full swing, supplies and equipment were rapidly building up ashore – the Lynx was landing and taking-off incessantly. The Flight Deck Officer reported, 'Lynx on deck, not ours, don't know who he is, I will find out.'

'Hope it's not Argie?' – quipped the Captain.

'Don't think so.'

A 'helo' from another ship had run into trouble.

The seat opposite the Captain was empty. Lieutenant Murphy, his Principal Weapons Officer (Air) was posted on the Gun Direction Position above the bridge. As the aircraft were coming in at low level, the ship would have to be fought visually, reverting to World War II tactics.

At 13.10 hours, Lt. Murphy heard a ship's siren wail from the Sound, then another, then all the ships took it up – the 'Argies' had arrived. Simultaneously, the Captain's voice came through his headphones.

'Enemy aircraft sighted in Sound. Look out west.'

The Action gong clanged – 'Air raid warning – Red.'

The LAZ Sight Operator turned to face west, peering through the LAZ Sight; the 4.5 inch gun automatically following, the pedestal sight at the back end would bring the close-range Seacat missiles to bear. Master at Arms, Locke, shouted down from the bridge to the extra look-outs on the upper deck. They pointed their seemingly useless weapons west – rifles, machine guns, 'Very' light pistols, smoke grenades, distress rockets, anything to distract the incoming Argie pilots and cause them to veer off. Hurtling in at 500 mph, a pilot has to react with split-second accuracy; in straight level flight, he has to release his bomb at a certain height and distance to score a hit. The slightest distraction or veering away will cause him to miss. Strapped to his 20mm Oerlikon anti-aircraft gun, Leading Seaman Walker swung round, aiming at the western hills.

'Aircraft sighted, bearing Red five zero' – a shouted report from the GDP. The peace was shattered as four Mirages flew screaming over the brow of the hill to swoop on the ships in 'Bomb Alley' – the Falkland Sound – and across San Carlos Water, which the 'Argies' were to know as 'Death Valley', with good reason. The pursuing Sea Harriers broke off to left and right at the crest of the hill, to avoid being caught in the flack. All hell broke loose. The ships opened up with everything. A deadly blanket crossfire of missiles, 4.5 inch shells, close range weapons, distress rockets and 'Very' light flares flew towards the attacking aircraft. L/S Walker on the Oerlikon pumped away at 800 yards, closing – swung round to follow the 'Argies' as they shrieked low over the ships. From the shore the Army put up a barrage of Rapier and Blowpipe (hand held) missiles. A bomb, released too low, skidding across the water, streaked past the *Arrow*; a towering column of water was flung up as another bomb exploded harmlessly in the sea. One Mirage exploded in mid-air, to plunge into the water a hundred yards away – everybody claimed the hit. The remaining three aircraft curved away, the rear one followed by a heat-seeking Rapier missile. There was a sudden flash from behind the hills – two down, two to go. The XO Lt. Commander Manning, from the bridge reported, 'Aircraft departing'. No one relaxed; no one was surprised at the Captain's 'Aircraft coming in again behind the mountains. Also we have reason to

believe raid coming in from south-west at 20 miles. Take track 4324 with gun.' Track 4324 was fed into the computer by 'Close Air' radar.

A minute later the two remaining Mirages, skimming the hill, hurtled in, 20 millimetres cannon spitting. Again the umbrella barrage, in seconds they were beyond the ships heading for home, one of the Mirages spewing smoke – that one was unlikely to get back to Argentina. With hardly a break the next raid was on them; feet only above the water, they screamed

in from the south-west – 4 – A4 Skyhawks. Two never reached the ships in San Carlos, the others dropped their bombs, missed and turned for home. The raids continued throughout the afternoon, pressed home with fanatical zeal – Argentina seemed willing to send in planes despite all losses. These were seldom less than 50% and sometimes a whole sortie failed to return to the homeland.

Against such onslaughts there had to be losses. Only the day before, the frigate *Antelope* had limped up the Bay trailing smoke, her main mast bent over at an angle, scythed by an Argentine plane, two gaping holes in her hull. Inside her had lain an unexploded bomb. After dark, at anchor, she exploded, hurling flaming debris high into the air. The unexploded bomb had gone off as they tried to defuse it. 'Helos'

and landing craft closed in to pick up survivors, ignoring the possibility of exploding ammunition. She burnt red-hot throughout the night and the following morning, finally slipping below the surface in a cloud of steam late in the afternoon.

The light was failing as the XO's voice came through the headphone, 'Land Rover, presumed friendly, passing down our starboard side at 400 feet, registration No. A3AM12.' The 'helos' had continued ferrying throughout the air attacks. The Captain went up to the bridge for a breath of fresh air, it was freezing cold, but still clear. A penguin unconcernedly waddled down the beach, almost within touching distance. Five Royal Marines sprang, as if by magic, from the ground and chased after it – it waddled faster and flopped into the water well ahead of its pursuers.

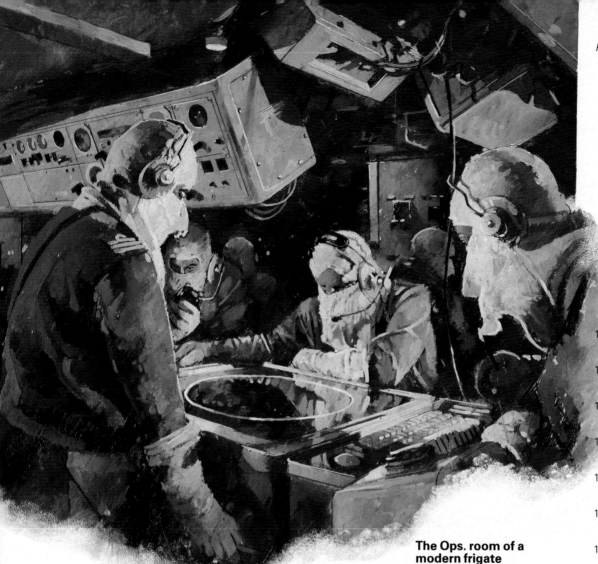

After dark the supply ships were escorted to safe waters. Now at defence stations, the crew of the *Arrow* sat down to a welcome hot meal. It was 22.45 hours. By 24.00 hours they were on their way to bombard an 'Argie' shore position. They were at action stations 18½ hours out of the 24 that day. Action stations – defence stations – action stations – this went on for 14 consecutive, tiring, weary days aboard all the frigates and destroyers covering the supply ships in San Carlos Water.

After the surrender on Tuesday, 15 June, Commander Bootherstone turned the *Arrow* into the Atlantic heading for home – relieved, but satisfied that the years of training had proved to be correct. More convinced than ever that the successful fighting of the ship had depended on each and every member of the ship's company – a team welded into an unbeatable fighting unit. From the engineers down below, to the LAZ Operator above the bridge, every man aboard had played an indispensable part in the victorious outcome of the operation. By the time they arrived in Devonport they had been continuously at sea for 101 days.

The Ops. room of a modern frigate

The Ops. room of a modern frigate is crowded with operators (21) and highly sensitive equipment.
There are 6 radar displays, each with its own computer keyboard.

A: Commanding Officer
B: Anti Submarine Warfare Director
C: Principal Warfare Officer
D: Operations Room Supervisor

Personnel and usual rank:

1   CO: Commanding Officer; PWO: Principal Warfare Officer
2   ORS: Operations Room Supervisor; Chief Petty Officer
3   ASWD: Anti Submarine Warfare Director; Petty Officer (Sonar)
4   ASWPS: Anti Submarine Warfare Picture Supervisor; Leading Seaman (Radar)
5   SC: Sonar Controller; Leading Seaman (Sonar)
6 & 7   OP: Sonar Operator; Able Seamen
8   GOPC: General Operations Plot Compiler; AB (Radar)
9   SPS: Surface Picture Supervisor; LS (Radar)
10   SPC: Surface Picture Compiler; AB (Radar)
11   AC(H): Aircraft Controller (Helicopter); PO (Radar)
12   AC(H)A: Aircraft Controller (Helicopter) Assistant; AB (Radar)
13   EW(D): Electronic Warfare (Director); PO(EW)
14   EW(OP): Electronic Warfare (Operator); AB(EW)
15   APR(L): Air Picture Reporter (Local); AB (Radar)
16   MD: Missile Director; CPO (GI)
17   MC1: Missile Controller 1; LS (Missile)
18   MC2: Missile Controller 2; PO (Missile)
19   APS: Air Picture Supervisor; AB (Radar)
20   CY: Communications Yeoman; Leading Radio Operator
21   RO(T): Radio Operator (Tactical)

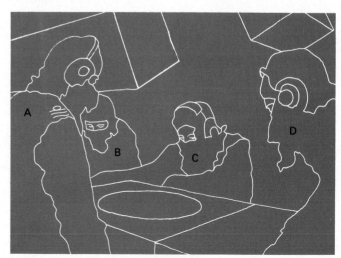

Combating an air attack in San Carlos Water

In the confined space of San Carlos Water, it was considered most likely that any attack would come from Argentinian aircraft, rather than surface ships or submarines. (San Carlos Water was too narrow and shallow for successful submarine operations.) This meant that most of the activity in the Ops. room was concerned with aircraft location and helicopter traffic control – although each radar display could, if necessary, cope with Air, Surface or Sub-Surface picture.

Information would come into the Ops. room in two ways:
1. From an outside source, via a link track (another ship picking up the radar track of approaching hostile aircraft would digitalize the information and send it by radio link. This would instantly be turned into a synthetic aircraft track, appearing on every radar display that was switched to air picture, the track carrying the identifying number of the ship sending the information).
2. By voice communication warning – 'Heads up, west.'

'Four A4 Skyhawks south-east, 30 miles, closing fast'. Sometimes these warnings would come in when the enemy were still 20 minutes, or even half an hour away.

Once the ship's own radar had locked on to the target and weapon systems alerted (fore, aft, or both), a decision had to be made to take it, either in manual control, or by a 'Hands off' method. This would leave the tracking to the computer entirely, which would decide to fire the missile when the enemy was at optimum intercept range. The whole action would be over in a matter of seconds.

Often, whilst at defence stations in San Carlos Water, the radar display would be cluttered by the nearby hills (as radar can only travel in a straight line, it bounces back from an obstruction and appears on the display), then, an aircraft track could pop up suddenly. The computer would decide whether or not it was a threat, if so, it would automatically select which weapon system to use and fire it. In which case, the missile would already be airborne when the klaxon blared out and the crew began rushing to action stations.

Missiles used during the Falklands Campaign

Exocet

Carried by frigates and destroyers – also used by Argentine Etendards. Exocet, which can be fired from either a ship or Super Etendard aircraft, travels from 6 to 10 feet above the water (making it difficult to detect by shipboard radar), at slightly under the speed of sound. The range and bearing of the target are fed into the missile's guidance system before launch, then it homes on to the target by radar.

Warhead: 352 pounds of high explosive
Length: 15 feet 4 inches
Body diameter: 1 foot 2 inches
Wing span: 3 feet 3½ inches
Weight at launch: 1,433 pounds
Speed: Mach 0.93
Range: 32 to 43 miles

Not to scale

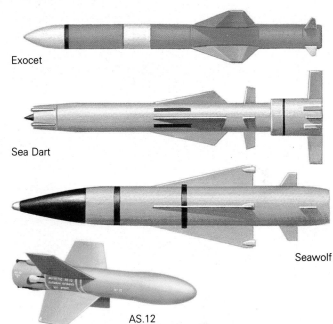

Exocet

Sea Dart

Seawolf

AS.12

Seacat

Sea Skua

Air-launched anti-ship missile fired from a Lynx helicopter

Warhead: 44 pounds high explosive
Length: 9 feet 3½ inches
Body diameter: 10½ inches
Weight at launch: 325 pounds
Maximum speed: slightly under the speed of sound
Maximum range: 8.7 miles

Sea Skua

Seawolf

Carried by Type 22 frigates. The Seawolf is either a surface-to-air, or surface-to-surface missile, capable of taking out aircraft and hostile missiles, using its fully automatic radar control and guidance.

Warhead: high explosive
Length: 6 feet 7 inches
Wing span: 2 feet 3½ inches
Weight at launch: 176 pounds
Maximum speed: supersonic

Seacat

Carried by frigates and destroyers, Seacat is a close-range anti-aircraft missile (surface-to-air) but can be used surface-to-surface. This missile is radio-controlled, either visually, by two men in a director, or by radar.

Warhead: high explosive
Length: 4 feet 10 inches
Body diameter: 7½ inches
Weight: 140 pounds
Maximum range: 3 miles

AS.12

Fired from Wasp and Wessex helicopters, this wire-guided air-to-surface missile, used mainly against fast patrol boats, has a range of 19,685 feet

Warhead: 62 pounds high explosive
Length: 6 feet 1.9 inches
Body diameter: 7 inches
Wing span: 2 feet 1½ inches
Weight at launch: 170 pounds
Speed at impact: 210 miles per hour
Maximum range: 19,685 feet

Sea Dart

Carried on ASW's (Anti-submarine and warfare aircraft carriers) and destroyers. These are ship-based surface-to-air and surface-to-surface missiles capable of intercepting aircraft and air-to-surface missiles.

Warhead: high explosive
Length: 14 feet 3½ inches
Body diameter: 1 foot 4½ inches
Span: 2 feet 11¾ inches
Weight at launch: 1,210 pounds
Range: at least 19 miles
Power: Rolls-Royce ram jet

Rank Insignia

Shoulder tabs: Great Britain

Admiral of
the Fleet

Admiral

Vice-
Admiral

Rear-
Admiral

Commodore
1st Class

Commodore
2nd Class

Captain

Commander

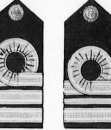
Lieutenant-
Commander

Lieutenant

Sub-Lieutenant

Warrant Officer

Midshipman

Cap badge:
Chief Petty
Officer

Cap badge:
Petty Officer

Sleeves: Great Britain

Admiral of
the Fleet

Admiral

Paymaster
Commander

Lieutenant-
Commander (RNVR)

Sub-Lieutenant
(RNVR)

Air Branch
Lieutenant Pilot

Air Branch Pilot

Sleeves: Germany

Rear-Admiral Line

Commodore Line

Korvettenkapitän Line

Kapitänleutnant Line

Leutnant

94

Shoulder tabs: Germany

Gross Admiral

General Admiral

Admiral

Vice-Admiral

Rear-Admiral Line

Rear-Admiral Engineering

Kapitan zur See Kommodore

Fregatten-kapitän

Korvetten-kapitän

Kapitän-leutnant

Oberleutnant zur See

Leutnant zur See

Fregatten-kapitän Ordnance

Marineassisten-zarzt Medical

Cap Badges

Italy

Tenente di Vascello Line

1st, 2nd and 3rd Chief Line

Germany

Officer

USA

Officer (post-1941)

International Code of Signals

 A

 B

 C

 D

 E

 F

 G

H

I

 J

K

L

 M

 N

O

 P

 Q

 R

 S

 T

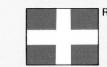 U

 V

 W

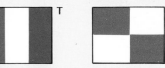 X

 Y

 1

 6

 Z

 2

7

 3

8

 4

9

 5

 0

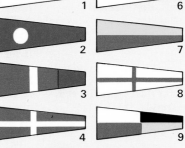

95

Index

Admiral Graf Spee, 36–7
aircraft at sea, 64–5, 70, 71; Albacore, 56–63; Avenger, 65; deck landing, 62–3, 64; helicopters, 84, 85, 88, 89, 93; Sea Harriers, 90; Short sea planes, 64, 65; Sopwith Strutter, 65; Swordfish, 56, 59, 60, 65, 71; vertical take off, 65; *Zero-Sen*, 65
aircraft carriers, 56–9, 65
Akagi, 65
Alfieri, 61
Alpino, 59
American Civil War at sea, 30–5
Antelope, HMS, 91
Antrim, HMS, 86, 87
Argentine air attack, San Carlos Water, 90–3
Argus, HMS, 65
Ark Royal, HMS, 64, 70, 71
Arrow, HMS, 84–92; guns, 88, 90; operations, 92

battles: Chesapeake, 30–5; Coronel, 41; Lepanto, 11; Midway, 65; Salamis, 4–9; San Carlos Water, 90–3; South Foreland, 10; Spanish Armada, 14–19; Trafalgar, 21–7
battleship, the, 36–7
bireme, 5
Bismarck, 36, 66–75; control armour, 72; gunnery, 68–9; routine, 74; sinking, 71–3, 75
Brilliant, HMS, 86
Bristol, HMS, 40
Bucentaure, 23, 24

Cadduci, 61
Carnarvon, HMS, 40
Cattaneo, Italian Vice Admiral, 61
'coaling ship', 41
Collingwood, Vice Admiral, 22
Cook, Captain, 17
Cornwall, HMS, 40
Crabbe, Commander, 80
Craddock, Rear Admiral Sir Christopher, 38, 41
Cunningham, Admiral Sir Andrew, 59

Daisy, 52
Dorsetshire, HMS, 71
Drake, Sir Francis, 12–14; and the Armada, 15–19
Dreadnought, HMS, 36
Dresden, 40, 42, 43

electronic warefare, 92
Ely, Eugene, 62, 64, 65
Emden, 40

Falklands: 1914, 38–43; 1982, 84–93
fighting ships: aircraft carrier, 56–63; ancient world, 4–9; battle ship, 36–7; clinker built, 10, 11; cog, 10; development of, 10–11; Falklands, 1982, 84–93; ironclads, 30–35; medieval, 10–11; Nelson's time, 20–27; Spanish Armada, 14, 17; steam, 30–36; Tudor, 11–12; World War I, 38–43; World War II, 45, 51–2, 56–61; *see also Bismarck*; submarines
fire ships, 16–17
Fiume, 61
Formidable, HMS, 56, 57, 62, 63
French Navy: battleships, 36; Trafalgar, 23–7
frogmen, 76–83

galleasses, 11, 14, 18
galleons, 14, 15, 17, 19
galleys, 4–9, 10, 14
German Navy: battleships, 36; World War I, 39–43; World War II, 44–52
Gioberti, 61
Glamorgan, HMS, 86
Glasgow, HMS, 38, 39, 41, 42, 43
Gneisenau, 40, 42, 43, 66
Golden Hind, 14
Good Hope, HMS, 40
Gosport speaking tube, 59, 60
Greek fighting ships, 4–9
guided missiles, 55, 65, 92; AS12, 93; Exocet, 85, 88, 93; Polaris, 55; Sea cat, 85, 93; Sea dart, 93; Sea skua, 93; Sea wolf, 93

Henry Grâce à Dieu, 11
Hermes, HMS, 84, 87, 88
Hitler, Adolf, 71
Holigost, 10
Holland, USS, 53, 55
Hood, HMS, 36, 66, 67, 68
Howard, Admiral Lord of Effingham, 15, 17
Hunley, CSS, 54

Iachino, Admiral Angelo, 59, 60
Inflexible, HMS, 40
Invincible, HMS, 42, 87
ironclads, 30–5, 36
Italian Navy: air attack on, 57–61; submarine activity, 76–82

Japanese Navy, 37, 39
Juno, HMS, 60

Kaiser Wilhelm, 11, 40
K-boats, 55
Kent, HMS, 40
King George V, HMS, 68, 71
Kriegsmarine *see* German Navy

La Gloire, 36
Leipzig, 41, 42, 43
life at sea: American Civil War, 31–5; *Arrow*, 85–92; *Bismarck*, 74; Drake's time, 13, 14, 16, 17; *Glasgow*, HMS, 38, 39, 41, 42, 43; scurvy, 17; steam, 30–3, 38–9, 43; surgery, 26; U-boats, 44, 45, 46, 48, 74; *Victory*, 21–27
Lucas, Captain, 24, 25, 27
Lutjens, Admiral, 67, 68, 70, 73

Madre de Dios, 13
Medina Sidonia, Duke of, 14, 17, 19
Merrimack, 30–32, 34–5
Minnesota, 32, 35
Monitor, 30–35
Monmouth, HMS, 40

Nautilus, 54
navigation, 25–9
Nelson, Admiral Lord, 21–27
New Jersey, 37
Norfolk, HMS, 66, 67, 68, 71
Nuestra Senora del Rosario, 15, 16
Nurnberg, 40, 42, 43

Oriani, 61
Otranto, 40, 41

Paixhans, Henri, 36
Pegasus, HMS, 52
Pelican, 12, 14
Peral, 54
Persian ships, 8
Plymouth, HMS, 86, 87
Pola, 60, 61
Popham's telegraphic code, 23
Prince of Wales, HMS, 66, 67, 68, 85
Prinz Eugen, 66, 67, 68

Queen Elizabeth, HMS, 76, 77, 81, 82

Redoutable, 24–7
Regent, 10
Renown, HMS, 70
Repulse, HMS, 52, 68, 85
Revenge, 12, 13, 15
Rodney, HMS, 71
Romans at sea, 10
Royal Oak, HMS, 45, 49, 50, 51, 52

San Lorenzo, 18
San Martin, 19
Scapa Flow, 44, 48, 50, 51, 52

Scharnhorst, 39–42
Scire, 76, 77, 82
Sheffield, HMS, 88
Short brothers aircraft, 64, 65
Spanish Armada, 14–19
Spee, Vice Admiral Maximillian Graf von, 39, 40, 41, 42
Sturdee, Vice Admiral Sir Doveton, 41, 42
submarine escape apparatus, 77
submarines: Browne's submersible, 53; De Son's submersible, 53; evolution of, 53–5; *George Washington*, 55; Italian, 76–7; K-boats, 55; midgets, 77–83; Plongeur Marin, 54; Sourcouf, 55; Turtle, 53; U-boats, 44–6, 48–9, 50–2, 55
Suffolk, HMS, 66, 67, 68

Themistokles, 4, 5, 6
Thunderer, HMS, 36
Tirpitz, 66
torpedoes: aerial, 56–60; manned, 77–84; on 'U47', 45, 49, 50, 51; US Mk13, 57, 58; Whitehead, 49
Tovey, Admiral, 70
trireme, 4–9

'U45', 44
'U47', 44, 45, 46, 47, 48
US navy: aircraft, 64–5; battleships, 37; submarines, 55

Valiant, HMS, 76, 77, 79, 80, 81, 82
Vanguard, HMS, 37
Victorious, HMS, 68
Victory, 20–7
victualling, 41
Viking longboat, 10, 28
Villeneuve, Vice Admiral, 23
Vittorio Veneto, 57, 59, 60

Warspite, HMS, 57, 59
weapons at sea: American Civil War, 30–35; ancient world, 8; battle ships, 37, 40; cannon, 10, 11, 15, 18, 19, 21–7; culverin, 14, 18, 19; fifteenth century, 10; gunnery on *Arrow*, 88, 90; on *Victory*, 25; guns at the Armada, 19; muskets, 19, 24, 25, 27; nineteen eighties, 92–3; sixteenth century, 11; *see also* guided missiles, torpedoes and specific ships

Yamoto, 37

Zara, 61